South East Scotland

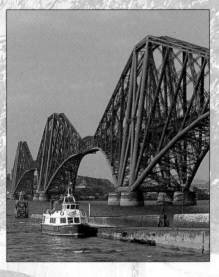

Car Tours

Neil Wilson

LEE GRAY   1998

Acknowledgements
The author would like to thank Carol Downie and Fiona MacIntyre for
their assistance in the preparation of this guide. Thanks also to Heather
Pearson and Ordnance Survey staff for painstakingly checking the maps
against the text.

Front cover photograph: *Killin and the Falls of Dochart*
Title page photograph: *Forth Rail Bridge*

While every care has been taken to ensure the accuracy of the route
directions, the publishers cannot accept responsibility for errors or
omissions, or for changes in details given. It is possible that road
numbers may have changed prior to publication. If readers know of
any changes which have taken place, or have noticed any inaccuracies,
Jarrold Publishing would be grateful to hear from them.

It also has to be emphasised that routes which are easy in fine
conditions may become hazardous during wet weather. Paths may
also become slippery, muddy and difficult. The publishers can take
no responsibility for incidents arising from following the routes.

Author: Neil Wilson
Series Editor: Anne-Marie Edwards
Editor: Hilary Hughes, Donald Greig
Designers: Brian Skinner, Visual Image
Photographs: Neil Wilson

Ordnance Survey   ISBN 0-3190-0631-X
Jarrold Publishing   ISBN 0-7117-0848-7

First published 1996 by Ordnance Survey and Jarrold Publishing

Ordnance Survey   Jarrold Publishing
Romsey Road   Whitefriars
Maybush   Norwich NR3 1TR
Southampton SO16 4GU

Printed in Great Britain by Jarrold Book Printing, Thetford, Norfolk 1/96

CONTENTS

KEY TO MAPS
• Inside •
front cover

KEY MAP
• page 4 •

AN INTRODUCTION TO SOUTHEAST SCOTLAND
• page 6 •

• TOUR 1 •

SOUTH SHORE OF THE FORTH, THE BATHGATE HILLS AND RATHO
• page 14 •

• TOUR 2 •

LINLITHGOW, THE UNION CANAL, CULROSS, CHARLESTOWN AND QUEENSFERRY
• page 18 •

• TOUR 3 •

THE CLYDE VALLEY: BIGGAR, LANARK AND TINTO HILL
• page 22 •

• TOUR 4 •

MIDLOTHIAN: CRAIGMILLAR, ROSLIN, CRICHTON AND DUDDINGSTON
• page 26 •

• TOUR 5 •

TWEED TO TALLA: PEEBLES, TRAQUAIR, ST MARY'S LOCH AND MEGGET
• page 30 •

• TOUR 6 •

THE BORDER ABBEYS, THE WOOL TOWNS AND SCOTT COUNTRY
• page 34 •

• TOUR 7 •

EAST LOTHIAN: HADDINGTON, EAST LINTON AND NORTH BERWICK
• page 38 •

• TOUR 8 •

THE LAMMERMUIR HILLS, DUNS AND DUNBAR
• page 42 •

• TOUR 9 •

ST ANDREWS AND CUPAR VIA THE EAST NEUK OF FIFE
• page 46 •

• TOUR 10 •

THE PENTLANDS, WEST LINTON, GLADHOUSE RESERVOIR AND NEWTONGRANGE
• page 50 •

• TOUR 11 •

STIRLING, THE OCHIL HILLS, DOLLAR AND CLACKMANNAN
• page 54 •

• TOUR 12 •

BANNOCKBURN, THE ANTONINE WALL AND THE CAMPSIE FELLS
• page 58 •

• TOUR 13 •

DUNFERMLINE, LOCH LEVEN, FALKLAND AND THE SOUTH FIFE COAST
• page 62 •

• TOUR 14 •

DUNBLANE, COMRIE, LOCH EARN AND CALLANDER
• page 66 •

• TOUR 15 •

CALLANDER, THE TROSSACHS AND THE LAKE OF MENTEITH
• page 70 •

• TOUR 16 •

A CIRCUIT OF STRATHEARN: GLEN ALMOND, CRIEFF, MUTHILL AND AUCHTERARDER
• page 74 •

• TOUR 17 •

ABERFELDY, GLEN LYON, BEN LAWERS AND LOCH TAY
• page 78 •

• TOUR 18 •

THE FIRTH OF TAY
• page 82 •

• TOUR 19 •

SCONE, BLAIRGOWRIE, PITLOCHRY AND DUNKELD
• page 86 •

• TOUR 20 •

DUNDEE, ARBROATH, BRECHIN AND GLAMIS CASTLE
• page 90 •

USEFUL ORGANISATIONS
• page 94 •

INDEX
• page 95 •

OS MAPS AND GUIDES
• Inside •
back cover

3

AN INTRODUCTION TO SOUTH EAST SCOTLAND

I f you take a pen to a map of Scotland and sketch a rough circle encompassing Stirling, Scone, St Andrews and Edinburgh, you will have outlined the country's historic heartland. Here were played out many of the battles and power struggles that shaped the fate of the nation, and here can be found many of its finest and most important historic monuments. Here too is a landscape of infinite variety, from the rolling farmland of East Lothian to the wild, heathered glens of the Ochil Hills, and from the rocky coast of Fife to the peaceful, wooded shores of the lochs of the Trossachs. The car tours described in this book are concentrated in this east-central heartland, exploring the history and landscape of Stirlingshire, Perthshire, Fife

Edinburgh Castle towers above the wooded walks of Princes Street gardens

Fife-Elie coastguard lookout

and the Lothians. In addition, there are routes which head south of Edinburgh into the Borders and upper Clydesdale, and others which extend north and west into the Trossachs and the fringes of the southern Highlands.

Geologically speaking, the Highlands are separated from Scotland's central valley by the Highland Boundary Fault, a deep fracture in the rocks that runs in a straight line across the country from southwest to northeast, passing through Loch Lomond, Comrie and Stonehaven. A similar, parallel fault runs from Girvan to Dunbar, marking the northern edge of the Border hills. The block of crust between these two faults has dropped down, leaving an area of younger and softer sedimentary rocks bounded by more resistant rocks to north and south. Differential erosion has resulted in the familiar geographical division of Scotland into the Highlands, the Central Lowlands, and the Southern Uplands.

But the central valley is not all low-lying. Intrusions of resistant volcanic rocks have created ranges of hills such as the Ochils, the Pentlands and the Campsie Fells, and smaller peaks such as North Berwick Law, the Bass Rock, Arthur's Seat and Largo Law. Many of these smaller rocky summits have been used throughout history as natural fortresses, as at Traprain Law, and most notably in the castle crags of Edinburgh and Stirling. Indeed, the landscape has played a vital part in influencing the history of this part of the country.

The easiest route for an army invading Scotland from the south has always been along the coastal plain of the Lothians, towards the bottleneck of Stirling, where anyone intent on penetrating further northwards had to squeeze between the tidal marshes of the Firth of Forth and the vast boggy plain of Flanders Moss to the west. The Romans came this way in the first century AD, and built their final frontier across the narrow waist of Scotland in the shape of the

Antonine Wall. The English followed in their footsteps in 1297, when Wallace stopped them at Stirling Bridge, and again in 1314, when Robert the Bruce awaited Edward's army above the route of the old Roman road at Bannockburn.

The Forth marked the southern boundary of the land of the Picts, the fearsome aboriginal tribes who halted the Roman advance two thousand years ago. The carved stones they left behind, bearing enigmatic symbols, hunting scenes and occasionally Christian crosses, are about the only evidence we have of these mysterious people. Another legacy is the profusion of place-names beginning with 'pit' (which is derived from pett, meaning a portion of land) in east and northeast Scotland, as in Pitlochry, Pitsligo and Pittenweem, to name but a few.

The Church of the Holy Rude sits on a hilltop above Stirling

Scotland north of the Forth was united into one kingdom in the ninth century when Kenneth MacAlpin, king of the Scots (descendants of Irish immigrants who lived in Argyll, on the west coast), usurped the Pictish throne. Kenneth made Scone his capital, established a cathedral at nearby Dunkeld, and brought with him from Argyll the Stone of Destiny, on which all Scottish kings were enthroned until 1296, when Edward I stole it and took it with him to England (where it sits to this day in Westminster Abbey). Despite this, Scone remained a place of coronation until Charles II became the last king to be crowned there in 1651.

Kenneth's successors extended their territory as far as the River Tweed, and the centre of Scottish power drifted southwards. Malcolm Canmore (c.1031–93) and Queen Margaret held court in Dunfermline and Edinburgh, and probably in Stirling too, where their son Alexander I died in 1124. Their youngest son, the pious David I (1084–1153), established many of the country's greatest abbeys and monasteries, including Dunfermline, Melrose, Holyrood, Jedburgh and Dryburgh, and also the houses of the Knights Templar (at Temple) and the Knights of St John (at Torphichen).

In the fifteenth and sixteenth centuries, under the Stewart kings, Edinburgh emerged as the political and cultural capital of Scotland, but there were also important royal palaces at Stirling, Linlithgow, Dunfermline and Falkland. St Andrews, with its magnificent cathedral, was the ecclesiastical capital of the country until the Reformation of 1560, when Protestant reformers inspired by John Knox rose up against the Catholic hierarchy. Many churches and monasteries were damaged or destroyed as Protestant zealots waged a campaign of destruction against the 'idolatrous' clergy.

The eighteenth century brought the Act of Union and the seat of political power moved south to Westminster. Scottish resentment surfaced in the Jacobite uprisings, the most famous of which was the one led by Bonnie Prince Charlie in 1745. Charles led his army of Highlanders south into England, occupying Perth and Edinburgh, and defeating a government army at Prestonpans, before being beaten back to defeat at Culloden the following year. The uprisings prompted the government to introduce a policy of pacification of the Highland clans, which required forts and garrisons, and a network of roads to serve them. The military roads and bridges constructed by General George Wade and others opened up the Highlands for the first time, and many of them still survive – Wade's Bridge at Aberfeldy, for example, and stretches of his roads in the Sma' Glen and at Dunkeld.

Geology played an important role in directing the industrial development of southeast Scotland in the nineteenth century. The

Talla Reservoir nestles among the Border hills to the south of Peebles

coalfields of Fife and the Lothians fuelled the
blast furnaces of Falkirk, which smelted iron
ore dug from the ground at Bo'ness. The
mines also fuelled the world's first oil
refinery at Bathgate, where James 'Paraffin'
Young distilled oil from the bituminous coal
and shale of West Lothian. Limestone was
processed in the kilns of Charlestown,
Middleton and Catcraig (near Dunbar) to
produce lime for agriculture and industry.

*The vaults of Dirleton
Castle in East Lothian*

With the arrival of the railways, Victorian
engineers were inspired to build some of the
most impressive industrial monuments of the nineteenth century,
including the Tay Railway Bridge and the spectacular Forth Bridge,
perhaps Scotland's most widely recognised landmark. The railways
also opened up the country to tourism, and many of the elegant
resorts which catered for Victorian tourists, such as Callander,
Pitlochry, North Berwick and Aberdour, continue to give pleasure to
present-day visitors.

From Castle to Country House

One of the most distinctive man-made features of the Scottish
landscape is the castle. The earliest fortifications in Scotland were the
hill forts or 'duns' of prehistoric tribes, whose earthworks can still be
seen on many hilltops throughout the country. These consisted of
little more than a rampart of turf with a timber palisade, in which the
people and their livestock could seek shelter in times of danger. A
more sophisticated defensive structure was the 'broch', a circular
wall of masonry with a small, easily blocked gate – these are fairly

*Fishing boats cram
into the little harbour
of Pittenweem, Fife*

common in the Highlands, but there is a good example in the Borders at Edenhall, near Abbey St Bathans.

The prototype of the typical Scottish castle was the 'motte and bailey', a flat-topped earthen mound surrounded by a ditch (or moat), and surmounted by timber buildings and a palisade. It was introduced by Norman knights who were granted lands by Scottish kings in the eleventh and twelfth centuries. Surviving mottes can be seen at Wolfclyde, near Biggar, and on the shore of Carron Valley Reservoir in the Campsie Fells.

In the thirteenth and fourteenth centuries the timber buildings were replaced by stone ones, and natural hills and outcrops were used instead of earthen mounds – the castle crags of Edinburgh and Stirling are good examples. The first stone castles were simple square towers, with an entrance on the first floor reached by a wooden stair that could be pushed away when under attack. These buildings must have been dark and gloomy as there were only a few small arrow slits for windows. But castles were not only defensive structures; they were also status symbols, designed to reflect the wealth and power of the local lord – the huge thirteenth-century round tower of Dirleton Castle, with its grand Lord's Chamber, is a good example.

The fourteenth century saw the emergence of the 'towerhouse', with four or five storeys and a rectangular or L-shaped floor plan. These had a cellar and pit prison in the basement, with the kitchens above, and a great hall above them. The upper storeys contained private bed chambers. Defensive measures included massive curtain walls, as at Tantallon and Doune; loophole windows for archers and crossbowmen; machicolations or projecting parapets with openings in the floor through which missiles could be dropped on attackers – Craigmillar Castle has extensive machicolations; and 'battered' walls

Dunkeld Cathedral enjoys a beautiful setting on the banks of the River Tay

with an outward-sloping section of masonry at the foot of the wall which kept attackers out from the wall and within easier reach of the defenders' missiles and arrows – St Andrews Castle is a good example.

The spread of peace and stability in the sixteenth and seventeenth centuries saw a change in emphasis from defence to comfort and style. Grand royal palaces such as Linlithgow and Falkland were built, and nobles experimented with the latest trends in architecture, such as the Italian-inspired courtyard façade at Crichton Castle. Gradually the fortress-castle evolved into the country house. In some cases (for example at Traquair and Glamis) the old towerhouse was incorporated into the new building, but more often the old towers were abandoned and grand new houses were erected with landscaped gardens and avenues, as in the elegant mansions of Hopetoun House and Kinross House.

The busy thoroughfare of Princes Street lies at the heart of Scotland's capital

Edinburgh

Few would deny that Scotland's capital is one of the most beautiful cities in Europe, set dramatically on a series of craggy hills overlooking the Firth of Forth. Its centrepiece is the beetling black crag of the Castle Rock, gouged and scoured by glaciers, and capped by one of the country's most imposing fortresses. The Castle Rock has been inhabited since at least 900 BC, when prehistoric tribes built their huts within the safety of its natural defences, but it was not until the time of the MacAlpin kings that it became the site of a royal residence. David I (1084–1153), the son of Malcolm Canmore, founded St Margaret's Chapel on the Rock's highest point, in memory of his mother, and David II (1324–71), son of Robert the Bruce, built himself a fine towerhouse on the site now occupied by the Half Moon Battery.

The castle was enlarged under the Stewart kings, acquiring a Royal Palace and a Great Hall, and Edinburgh soon became the effective capital of Scotland. The Crown Jewels and the state records were kept safe in the castle, and the Scottish parliament met either here or in the Tolbooth on the Royal Mile, and later in the purpose-built Parliament House, now the home of the Scottish Law Courts. The city's status was enhanced by the building of the Palace of Holyroodhouse, which was begun by James IV and James V, and extended during the seventeenth century.

Greyfriars Bobby – a well-known Edinburgh landmark

The development of Edinburgh over the centuries can be seen in the view from the castle: the Old Town tenements on the Royal Mile, watched over by the late fifteenth-century crown spire of St Giles; the eighteenth-century New Town on the ridge to the north; and the Victorian suburbs of Marchmont and Morningside spreading southwards towards the Pentland Hills. There is so much to see in Edinburgh that even a long weekend would not be enough to cover it all. Apart from the main attractions of the Castle, the Royal Mile, and the Palace of Holyroodhouse, there are the collections of the Royal Museum of Scotland, the Scottish National Portrait Gallery and the National Gallery; the picture-postcard 'villages' of Cramond, Dean and Swanston; the wooded avenues of the Royal Botanic Gardens, and the penguin parade at Edinburgh Zoo; delightful walks on Calton Hill, Arthur's Seat and the Pentlands – the list goes on and on. For those wishing to explore this fascinating city, further information can be obtained from the Edinburgh and Scotland Information Centre in Waverley Market (see p. 94).

ENJOY YOUR TOUR

Please read through the tour before starting, and if visibility is poor when you intend to set out then reject one that offers fine panoramas from lofty viewpoints in favour of a neighbouring route that visits historic buildings or towns. Note that all routes are circular so they can be started at any point. Tour instructions are in bold type. There are also boxed letters which correspond to those on the map. Their purpose is to aid your navigation and, in many instances, highlight sections of the route requiring particular attention. The times given for each tour cover motoring only; if you decide to explore footpaths or visit attractions, they can easily take the best part of a day. The opening times of the various attractions can change, and you are advised to telephone and check before visiting. If you plan more extensive walks the Pathfinder guides and Pathfinder maps at 1:25,000 scale (2½ inches to 1 mile, 4cm to 1km) are ideal. For details see inside back cover.

In order to explore some of the loveliest areas of southeast Scotland many of the routes here follow narrow roads with steep gradients. Some cross high ground and may be blocked by drifting snow or made hazardous by ice in winter (gritting trucks rarely venture off the main roads). Obviously, driving on minor roads in hill country presents problems not encountered elsewhere. It is always best to assume that there is a slow-moving tractor just around the next bend, and to keep a lookout for sheep or cattle that might stray onto the (often unfenced) road. Never trust roadside sheep and lambs who may appear to be preoccupied with grazing – they are likely to amble across the road at the last minute. And finally, if you are sightseeing on a single-track road, please remember to pull over into the passing places as often as possible to allow following traffic to pass.

SOUTH SHORE OF THE FORTH, THE BATHGATE HILLS AND RATHO

54 MILES – 2½ HOURS
START AND FINISH IN EDINBURGH

The lands of West Lothian are rich in history, from the prehistoric burial chambers of Cairnpapple Hill, to the stately homes of Hopetoun House and Dalmeny. This tour follows the south shore of the Firth of Forth as far as the old steam railway at Bo'ness, then heads inland to the Bathgate Hills, from whose summits you can see both sides of the country, from Arran in the west to North Berwick in the east. The return leg goes by way of the Union Canal at Ratho.

Take the A90 out of Edinburgh (Queensferry Road), following signs for the Forth Road Bridge. As you leave Edinburgh, the road crosses the River Almond at the Cramond Brig Hotel, which overlooks old Cramond Brig, built in 1622. On the old bridge's wooden predecessor, James V, travelling incognito, was rescued from thieves by the local miller, Jock Howieson. His family was granted land in return, on the condition that there should always be someone to offer a basin and jug

of water whenever a monarch crosses the bridge. The promise was kept on several occasions, most recently in 1952 when Elizabeth II made a visit to the city of Edinburgh. **Two miles after the Barnton Roundabout, leave the dual carriageway onto the B924 to Dalmeny and South Queensferry. After half a mile you reach the entrance to Dalmeny House on the right.**

As you leave Dalmeny Estate, cross the B924 and take the road opposite the

entrance to reach the village of Dalmeny. The village was built to house workers on the Dalmeny Estate, but it contains what is perhaps the best-preserved Romanesque church in the country. Dating from the twelfth century, and dedicated to St Cuthbert, it has a beautiful south door decorated with grotesque faces and an interlaced arcade of five arches. Inside is the massive, carved stone coffin of an unknown person, perhaps the founder. **Turn right just past the old church in the middle of the village.** There is an impressive end-on view of the Forth Bridge ahead. **Then turn left at a T-junction onto the B924, and head downhill into South Queensferry.**

Follow Main Street through South Queensferry and up the hill at the far end, and as you pass beneath the Forth Road Bridge turn right towards Hopetoun House. The road runs along the shore before passing through a gateway and along an impressive avenue to the parking area in front of the house (tickets from the kiosk at left). **Leave Hopetoun House via the little estate road between the**

The harbour at South Queensferry

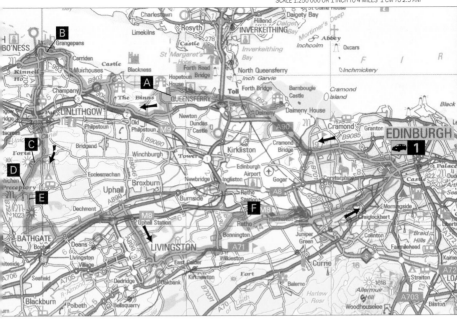

ticket kiosk and the Garden Centre **A**. You pass the estate office, go over a cattle grid, and through tree-dotted cattle pastures to reach the western entrance. **At the exit, turn left, then right at a row of cottages, and right again at the A904 towards Linlithgow.** After two miles you will see a tower on a ridge to your right, and then the entrance to the House of the Binns (National Trust for Scotland). The House of the Binns is the family seat of the Dalyell family, and dates from the seventeenth century (though much altered since). It was the first property to be acquired by the National Trust for Scotland (in 1944) and is notable for its fine Italian-style plasterwork. It takes its name from its hilltop site overlooking the Forth, 'binns' being a corruption of the old Scots *bynnis*, meaning 'hills'. **Immediately after the House of the Binns entrance turn right on the B9109, then right at the next T-junction to reach Blackness and its forbidding castle.** In the sixteenth century Blackness was one of the busiest harbours on the Forth (it was the port for Linlithgow Palace) but today it is a quiet village with a

• PLACES OF INTEREST •

Dalmeny House
Built in 1815 for the fourth Earl of Rosebery, Dalmeny House was the first Scottish example of neo-Gothic styling. It sits on a low rise above the sea, with a grand view of the Firth of Forth and the islands of Cramond and Inchcolm. Dalmeny is the private home of the present Earl and Countess of Rosebery; the guided tour leads you through several of the magnificent public apartments, containing the famous Rothschild Mentmore collection of eighteenth-century French furniture, porcelain and tapestries, together with paintings by Gainsborough, Raeburn and Reynolds. There is also a Napoleon Room which contains an

important collection of material associated with the Emperor, collected by the fifth Earl (who was Britain's Prime Minister from 1894 to 1895).
    Open May–September, Sundays 1–5.30, Mondays and Tuesdays 12–5.30. Telephone: (0131) 331 1888.

South Queensferry
This attractive town curves along the steep shore beneath the southern ends of the Forth bridges, with a distinctive terraced High Street and a fine medieval church. Just west of the little harbour, a commemorative plaque marks 'The Binks', the natural rock ledge where the original

'Queen's Ferry' (see Tour 2) used to land. At the western edge of the town, beneath the rail bridge, is the Hawes Inn (established 1683), where David Balfour's fate was sealed in Robert Louis Stevenson's novel *Kidnapped*. The history of the town and the building of the bridges are described in the little museum in the High Street.
    Queensferry Museum. Open Monday, Thursday, Friday and Saturday 10–1; Sundays 2.15–5. Telephone: (0131) 331 1590.
    Inchcolm. Boat trips depart from the pier beside the Hawes Inn for Inchcolm island (see Tour 13). Daily sailings June–September, weekends only April–May. Telephone: (0131) 331 4857.

House of the Binns
Open May–October, daily
1.30–5.30; closed Fridays.
Grounds open all year, daily 10–7.
Telephone: (0150 683) 4255.

Blackness Castle
The royal fortress of Blackness,
built in the fifteenth and sixteenth
centuries on a sea-girt promontory
in the Firth of Forth, is one of the
most formidable strongholds in
Scotland. It was designed to
withstand the worst bombardment
that contemporary artillery could
deliver, and has been the property
of the Crown since 1453, serving
as state prison, garrison and
ammunition depot. In plan it is
shaped roughly like a ship
pointing out to sea, and at either
end you will find the Stem and the
Stern towers.

Open April–September,
Monday–Saturday 9.30–6.30,
Sundays 2–6.30; October–March,
Monday–Saturday 9.30–4.30,
Sundays 2–4.30; closed Thursday
afternoons and Fridays.
Telephone: (01506) 834807.

**Bo'ness and Kinneil Steam
Railway**
A paradise for railway buffs, the
old Bo'ness station has been
converted into a working museum
and exhibition by the Scottish
Railway Preservation Society. You
can buy a ticket for a steam train
excursion to the Birkhill Fireclay
Mine, another industrial museum,
about 4 miles down the line. Open
daily July–mid August, weekends
only April–mid October, and at
other selected times (call for
details). Five departures daily,
between 11.30 and 4.30.
Telephone: (01506) 822298.

Hopetoun House
This is surely the grandest of all
Scotland's stately homes, an Adam
mansion created in the mid-
eighteenth century for Sir Charles
Hope, first Earl of Hopetoun.
Although the house is now owned
by a charitable trust, part of it is
still the home of the Earl's
descendants (now Marquises of
Linlithgow). There are guides on
hand, but you are free to wander at
will through the splendid
apartments, in which much of the
original eighteenth-century
furnishings survive. The
centrepiece is the magnificent
wood-panelled staircase, carved
with flowers and foliage, beneath a
cupola with frescoes depicting the
apotheosis of the Hope family. The
extensive grounds contain
woodland walks and picnic tables,
as well as exhibitions on history
and wildlife.

Open Easter–September, daily
10–5.30. Telephone: (0131) 331
2451.

nice pub and a sandy beach, and
the only boats to be seen in the
bay are local yachts.

On leaving Blackness
follow the signs for Bo'ness,
and turn right at the junction
with the A904. At the edge of
town turn right (signposted
'Tourist Information' and
'Steam Railway') and follow
this road into the centre of
Bo'ness. About a hundred
yards past a prominent
gasometer on the right, turn
right down a side street
(signposted 'Steam Railway')
B, and right again into the
car park for the Bo'ness and
Kinneil Steam Railway. In the
eighteenth century Bo'ness (or
Borrowstounness, to give it its full
name) was a thriving harbour
town, dealing in coal and salt, and
trading with France and Holland.
It declined after the opening of
the Forth and Clyde Canal in
1790, and the development of the
harbour at Grangemouth. Its
huge, deserted harbour now lies
full of mud, unused except for the
occasional visiting yacht at the
outer quay.

Leave the car park and go
straight on, parallel to the
railway line. At a small
roundabout take the
Grangemouth road (fourth
exit), to a T-junction where
you turn left uphill, past the
entrance to Kinneil House.
The grounds of Kinneil House
have several attractions: the
Kinneil Museum with displays of
local history, including locally
produced cast iron and pottery,

Hopetoun House

and Roman finds from excavations along the nearby Antonine Wall (see Tour 12); and James Watt's workshop cottage where the inventor worked on the prototype of his revolutionary steam engine. **At the traffic lights beyond, turn right onto the A706 towards Linlithgow.** Linlithgow is described in Tour 2. **At the T-junction in Linlithgow turn right and then immediately left towards Beecraigs Country Park. The road climbs into the Bathgate Hills and soon after entering the trees reaches the Cockleroy car park on the right** . From here, a short and easy walk through the woods leads to the summit of Cockleroy (912 feet, 278m) which affords a fine view over Linlithgow and the Firth of Forth. On a clear day you can see Ben Vorlich and Stuc a' Chroin in the Highlands to the north, the Isle of May and North Berwick Law to the east and, if you are lucky with the weather, the peaks of Arran in the west.

Just over a mile beyond the car park, opposite a lay-by **D**, a very narrow road on the right winds its way down to Torphichen. **Take the first road on the left as you enter the village to find the Torphichen Preceptory.** This fortified medieval church and towerhouse was the Scottish seat of the Knights Hospitaller of St John of Jerusalem, an order of warrior-monks founded in the Holy Land during the Crusades. The Preceptory was established in the late twelfth century, and now houses a fascinating exhibition explaining the history of the Order. **Turn left at the T-junction beyond the Preceptory, then left again (sign for Cairnpapple Hill), and climb uphill. Just after merging with another road coming in from the right, turn right and right again up a steep hill to a parking place beneath some trees, with a wooden gate leading to**

Bo'ness & Kinneil Railway

Cairnpapple Hill E. This great cairn is the most important prehistoric archaeological site in Scotland, with evidence of ritual observances, cremations and burials extending from 2500 BC to the first century AD. Information boards and reconstructions help to make sense of the remains.

Continue past Cairnpapple Hill and beneath a lookout point on the left (parking is available on far side), then downhill to a T-junction. Go left and then after one mile turn right at some cottages, then left on the A89 towards Broxburn. Go straight across at two roundabouts, then right at the traffic lights on the B8046 towards Pumpherston. The route passes through the region of West Lothian where the British oil industry was born, when in 1850 James 'Paraffin' Young began mining and refining the local oil shale to produce paraffin. The legacy of the oil shale industry is a landscape of spoil heaps, or 'bings', made up of the spent, pale pink shale. **Cross the bridge to**

Mid Calder, then go left onto the B7015 across a second bridge into East Calder. At the A71 turn left into village of Wilkieston, where the route goes left down the B7030 before turning right at Bonnington Mains Farm to the pretty canal-side village of Ratho. The village, which has a twelfth-century parish kirk, was once a quarry-workers town, and a staging post on the Union Canal (see Tour 2). It has a fine inn, where you can enjoy a meal on one of the restaurant barges that cruise along the canal to the Almond Aqueduct, or take a picnic and walk along the towpath.

From the canal, return along the same way you came but turn left at the post office **F**, then go first left, crossing the canal after a mile, and passing the Suntrap Gardening Advice Centre, before reaching a T-junction. A right turn here leads back to the A71, which will take you back into the centre of Edinburgh. ■

LINLITHGOW, THE UNION CANAL, CULROSS, CHARLESTOWN AND QUEENSFERRY

**46 MILES – 2 HOURS
START AND FINISH IN LINLITHGOW**

Since at least the sixteenth century, the livelihoods of many Forth valley communities were based on coal, oil-shale, limestone and salt. Most of these industries have died out, but their legacy is still visible in the landscape and the towns that line the shores of the Firth of Forth. This tour makes a circuit of the upper estuary, combining the historic sites of Linlithgow and Culross with the industrial heritage of West Lothian and Fife. It also visits two of the greatest achievements of nineteenth-century civil engineers: the Union Canal and the Forth Bridge.

Turn right out of the square below Linlithgow Palace, heading west on the A803 towards Falkirk. At the edge of town, immediately after crossing the bridge over the River Avon, turn left at the Bridge Inn on the B825 to Avonbridge. After about a mile or so the road crosses the Union Canal. From here it is a short walk along the towpath to the Avon

Aqueduct, a 12-arched masterpiece of civil engineering that carries the canal 86 feet above the River Avon. There is a car park a few hundred yards beyond the bridge at Muiravonside Country Park, which has woodland walks leading to the canal and the river. **Just over a mile beyond the canal you reach a roundabout A. Go right on the B805**

towards Polmont. The route now passes through the suburbs of Falkirk, and crosses over the canal again before reaching the main road. **At the junction with the main road A803 in Polmont, turn left. At the roundabout go straight across to visit Callendar House and Falkirk, but to follow the route, go right. Go straight across the next**

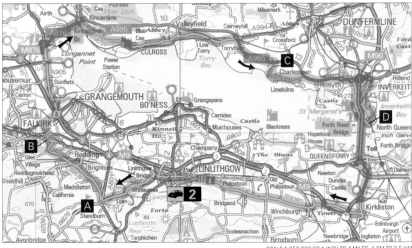

SCALE 1:250 000 OR 1 INCH TO 4 MILES *1 CM TO 2.5 KM*

roundabout, then go right onto the A904. At the motorway intersection (M9, junction 6) take the second exit (signposted A905 Stirling). The road crosses the River Carron, whose waters once provided power for the bellows for the Carron Iron Works' blast furnaces, and heads across the flat flood plain of the River Forth. This area has long been the industrial heart of the Forth valley, and even though the iron works and the mines have now closed down, the flares of Grangemouth oil refinery and the chimneys of Kincardine and Longannet power stations across the river are constant reminders.

Go straight across one roundabout, then turn right onto the A876 at the next one, and cross the River Forth on Kincardine Bridge. The bridge was opened in 1936, at which time it was the lowest bridging point on the Forth (a distinction it ceded to the Forth Road Bridge in 1964). The central section used to swing sideways to allow large ships to pass, but since 1988 it has been permanently closed. At the far side of the Forth you enter Kincardine. Turn right beside the clock tower on the B9037 to Culross. At a T-junction turn right then immediately left (follow brown Tourist Route signs for Culross).
Longannet Power Station, whose massive bulk and 600-foot chimney dominate the skyline, is the largest power station in Britain. Its four 600-megawatt generators produce half of the electricity used in central Scotland. Beyond Longannet the scenery becomes more rural, as befits the approach to the Royal Burgh of Culross, one of the Forth's most historic villages. This is the legendary birthplace of the sixth-century St Kentigern (also known as St Mungo, the patron saint of Glasgow), and the site of a Cistercian abbey, founded in 1217. The town made a living from salt-panning, coalmining

Linlithgow

The former county town of West Lothian enjoys an attractive setting on the south shore of Linlithgow Loch, dominated by the massive shell of Linlithgow Palace, the town's original raison d'être. The palace was built during the fifteenth and sixteenth centuries on the site of a royal manorhouse, and was a favourite residence of Scottish monarchs. James V was born here in 1512, as was his daughter Mary Queen of Scots in 1542. Unfortunately, the building was gutted by fire after being set alight by the Duke of Cumberland's troops in 1746, as they harried the retreating Jacobite army of Prince Charles Edward Stuart. The palace is now a roofless shell, but impressive and atmospheric nonetheless.

Next to the palace stands St Michael's Parish Church, capped with a distinctive and controversial aluminium spire that was added in 1964 (the old stone crown spire was in a dangerous condition). James IV is said to have seen a ghost in the church in 1512, that warned him of coming defeat at Flodden.

Linlithgow Palace. Open April–September, Monday–Saturday 9.30–6.30, Sundays 2–6.30; October–March, Monday–Saturday 9.30–4.30, Sundays 2–4.30. Telephone: (01506) 842896.

Union Canal

Work on the canal began in 1817, with the intention of providing cheap transport to carry coal from central Scotland to markets in Edinburgh, and it was opened in 1822. As well as carrying coal, there were several horsedrawn passenger barges a day, but soon after opening it was rendered obsolete by the expansion of the railways. It is a contour canal – it follows a constant height from one end to the other – and runs for $31^{1}/_{2}$ miles from central Edinburgh to Falkirk, where a flight of locks (now filled in) allowed barges to descend to the Forth and Clyde Canal and so to Glasgow. It crosses four aqueducts, including the spectacular Avon Aqueduct just west of Linlithgow, and near Falkirk it passes through a 700 yard (640m) tunnel. At the canal basin in Linlithgow there is a museum, housed in a row of cottages, which illustrates the canal's history. You can hire rowing boats here, or take a cruise along the canal in a steam launch, or explore the waterside wildlife on a walk along the towpath.

Union Canal Museum and Boat Trips, Manse Road Basin, Linlithgow. Open Easter–September, weekends only 2–5. Telephone: (01506) 842575.

Linlithgow Palace

Falkirk

The down-to-earth town of Falkirk may seem an unlikely tourist attraction but it has a long and fascinating history. The Antonine Wall runs through the middle of town, with a well-preserved 400-yard stretch visible in Callendar Park, later the site of the Battle of Falkirk (1298), in which the English took revenge on William Wallace for their defeat at Stirling Bridge the previous year. In the early nineteenth century, nearby Stenhousemuir was the site of Britain's largest annual cattle tryst, when over 600,000 head of cattle and sheep, and half a million pounds, changed hands each year. Here too was the famous Carron Iron Works, which produced the parts for James Watt's steam engine and the guns for Nelson's navy. Founded in 1759, it finally closed in 1982.

Callendar House, a splendid nineteenth-century chateau set in a lovely wooded park on the edge of town, houses a working Georgian kitchen, an exhibit describing the house's evolution from the fourteenth century to the present day, and (in preparation) a museum recording life in Falkirk during its industrial heyday between 1750 and 1850. The grounds include a boating lake and picnic area. Open Monday–Saturday 10–5, Sundays 2–5 (April–September only). Telephone: (01324) 612134

Culross

This historic village is the country's best-preserved example of a small Scottish town of the seventeenth century. The main buildings are the Town House, built in 1626 (the tower was added in 1783), which now houses an exhibition illustrating 400 years of the town's history; and the Palace, the house of the wealthy local merchant George Bruce, built between 1597 and 1611, with beautifully painted timber beams and ceilings. Open Good Friday–September, daily 11–5 (Palace) and 1.30–5 (Town House). Telephone: (01383) 880359.

Deep Sea World

Opened in 1993, this state-of-the-art marine aquarium includes a moving walkway which carries visitors through a transparent underwater viewing tunnel, surrounded by schools of cod, pollack and coalfish, where you can get a close-up view of sharks, rays and huge conger eels. Other exhibits include a touch-pool, where you get the opportunity to handle various sea creatures, and tanks displaying native Scottish marine life and coral reef fish. Open April–October, daily 9.30–6 (7 in July and August); November–March, Monday–Friday 10–4, weekends 10–6. Telephone: (01383) 411411.

and trade with the Low Countries, but decline set in during the eighteenth century. It was saved by the National Trust for Scotland, whose restoration programme has preserved the cobbled lanes and crow-stepped gables of the sixteenth and seventeenth centuries.

Continue through Culross, Valleyfield and Torryburn. At a roundabout, turn right on the A985 to Inverkeithing. After 2 miles (3.3km) turn right into Charlestown .
This was a model community laid out the 1750s by Charles, the fifth Earl of Elgin, to quarry and calcine the limestone that outcropped on his land. The village is arranged around a large green, with the (now exhausted) quarries on the wooded ridge above, overlooking the limekilns and the harbour, from which the cut stone and processed lime were exported all over the country. Stone from Charlestown was used to build the harbours at Leith and Dundee. **Continue along the seafront through Limekilns and back to the A985 where the route turns right.** Down to the right you can see Rosyth Naval Dockyard, which was established in 1903 and closed down in 1995.

Go straight across one roundabout, and bear right at the next on the B980/981 to North Queensferry. This village, and its companion on the south shore, take their names from Queen Margaret, wife of the eleventh-century Scots king Malcolm Canmore, who guaranteed free passage across the Forth for pilgrims on their way to St Andrews. The 'Queen's Ferry' continued to make the crossing until 1964, when the opening of the Forth Road Bridge finally made it obsolete. The railway bridge, which is known simply as 'the Forth Bridge', is one of Scotland's best-known landmarks, and the ultimate masterpiece of Victorian engineering. One and a half miles

Callendar House in Falkirk

(2.4km) long and carrying the railway line 150 feet (46m) above the water, it was built between 1883 and 1890, and took 55,000 tons (55,885 tonnes) of steel, 8 million rivets and the lives of 57 men. The area to be painted amounts to 135 acres (55 hectares), and the expression 'like painting the Forth Bridge' is still applied to any seemingly endless task. Nestled in a flooded quarry beneath the north end of the bridge is the marine aquarium of Deep Sea World.

At the far end of the harbour, just before the turn off to Deep Sea World, go left up the very steep and narrow Ferry Hills Road D. At the T-junction beyond the railway bridge turn right into Inverkeithing. Although it is now a dirty industrial port, the harbour of Inverkeithing has a long history and is said to have sheltered the Roman galleys of Agricola in the first century AD. The town itself was made a royal burgh in 1165, and a few historic buildings survive, including part of a Franciscan friary which now houses the Burgh Museum. **Continue through the town to a roundabout, and turn left.**

The Town House at Culross

At the next intersection, exit left to cross the Forth Road Bridge.

Take the first exit left after the toll booths, and at the intersection exit left on the A8000 (signposted M8/M9). At the next two roundabouts go straight across towards Kirkliston, on the B800. Kirkliston's claim to fame is the distillery where the famous liqueur Drambuie is made. The factory is modern, but the recipe is over 250 years old, and is said to have been entrusted to the Mackinnon family by none other than Bonnie Prince Charlie. **At the traffic lights in Kirkliston turn right on the B9080 to Winchburgh and Linlithgow.** The route returns to the Union Canal at Winchburgh, a former shale-mining town whose history is evident in the enormous bings that rise all around, and runs parallel to it through the attractive little villages of Threemiletown, Bridgend and Kingscavil. On the canal bank near Kingscavil is one of the old stables that once sheltered the barge horses. **Follow the B9080 back into Linlithgow.**

The Forth Bridges

THE CLYDE VALLEY: BIGGAR, LANARK AND TINTO HILL

52 MILES – 2½ HOURS
START AND FINISH IN BIGGAR

The upper reaches of the River Clyde wind around the heathery slopes of Tinto Hill, the region's most prominent landmark, before plunging into the rocky gorge of Corra Linn. At New Lanark, beside the waterfalls, David Dale and Robert Owen built a unique cotton-milling community that has been preserved as one of Britain's top tourist attractions. This tour begins in the pleasant country town of Biggar, and follows the Clyde as it loops around Tinto, before returning through the historic lands of the Douglas Water valley.

On Biggar High Street, head downhill and out of town towards Carlisle. Fork right on the A72 heading towards Glasgow. Less than a mile later, turn right at Wolfclyde Bridge. The bridge spans the River Clyde, the third longest river in Scotland after the Tay and the Spey. It flows for over 100 miles from the slopes of the Lowther Hills to Glasgow, passing through some of Scotland's richest agricultural land before mingling with the sea in the city that once boasted the biggest shipbuilding industry in the world. At this point the river is a swift and shallow stream, popular with trout anglers. On the far bank, near the bridge, is a fine example of a Norman motte, the manmade mound on which a timber fortification once stood. Ahead rises the little conical hill called Quothquan Law, topped with the earthworks of a prehistoric fort. **Where the road forks beneath Quothquan Law, bear right Ⓐ. Turn right at a T-junction into Quothquan village, then take the first road on the left, signposted Libberton.** The Clyde, off to the left of the road, now becomes more sluggish and begins to meander around the low mound of Cairngryffe Hill, before rushing headlong through the gorge below Lanark. **Turn left at a T-junction onto the B7016.** The route now passes through the remote hamlet of Libberton and crosses the level flood plain of the Clyde and its tiny tributary the Medwin Water, before climbing up to Carnwath on the edge of the moor. **At the T-junction in Carnwath, turn left onto the A721.**

Carnwath village hides a few

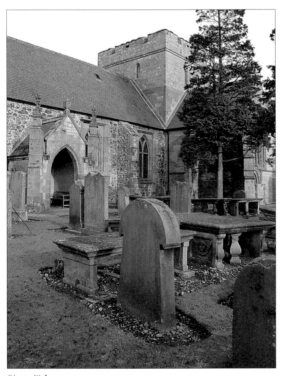

Biggar Kirk

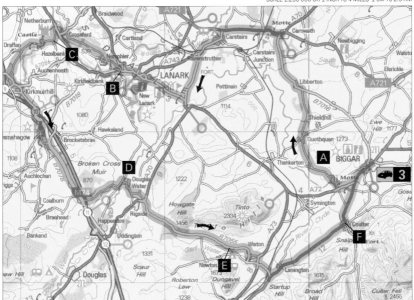

SCALE 1:250 000 OR 1 INCH TO 4 MILES *1 CM TO 2.5 KM*

historical delights. Besides the temptations of the Wee Bush Inn, a thatched pub where Robert Burns once downed a few whiskies, there is the sixteenth-century Mercat Cross, and the transept of a fifteenth-century collegiate church which survives at the west end of the newer parish kirk. As you leave the village you will see a wooded mound on the golfcourse to the right of the road. This is actually another Norman motte, possibly built by the ancestors of the Sommerville family who founded the collegiate church.

The road between Carnwath and Carstairs passes through a landscape of grass-covered ridges, composed of sand and gravel deposits that are being actively quarried. These ridges are known as kames and eskers, and they were originally laid down by glacial streams flowing under and around the edges of the retreating ice sheet at the end of the last Ice Age, about 13,000 years ago. **Two and a half miles**

• PLACES OF INTEREST •

Biggar
The town of Biggar, with its pretty little sixteenth-century church, sits by a gap in the hills where the ancient route linking the valleys of the Clyde and the Tweed passes through. It is only a small town, providing shops and services for the surrounding farms, but it has more museums to its name than many places ten times its size. A close (beside The Crown pub) leads from the broad High Street to the Gladstone Court Museum, whose name reminds us that the grandfather of the former British Prime Minister William Gladstone came from Biggar. The museum recreates a nineteenth-century street, where you can wander into the bank, the school or the library, and visit the premises of a grocer, a dressmaker or a photographer, to name but a few. Nearby is the Greenhill Covenanters' House, a seventeenth-century farmhouse dismantled and rebuilt in Biggar, and now serves as a museum of rural life, with a special emphasis on the Covenanters. The Moat Park Heritage Centre, housed in a former church on the main street, illustrates the history of the Upper Clyde and Tweed valleys from prehistoric times to the present day, while the Biggar Gasworks Museum comes complete with working machinery, gas lamps and steam engines.
Gladstone Court Museum. Open Easter–October, Monday–Saturday 10–12.30 and 2–5, Sundays 2–5. Telephone: (01899) 21050.
Moat Park Heritage Centre. Open Easter–October, Monday–Saturday 10–5, Sundays 2–5. Telephone: (01899) 21050.

Lanark
The busy market town of Lanark has a distinguished history, but unfortunately there is little left to see. The church at the foot of the High Street has a statue of William Wallace who once lived nearby. Wallace began his rebellion here, by killing the English sheriff and overthrowing the garrison, in revenge for the murder of his wife. The granting of royal burgh status in 1140 is still remembered each year in the traditional Lanimer festival and the Riding of the Marches which culminates in a colourful procession of decorated carnival floats and the crowning of the Lanimer Queen on the second Thursday in June.

23

beyond Carnwath, turn left on the A70 to Ayr. Carstairs, an attractive village set around a central green, is probably best known for the nearby Carstairs Junction, where the railway lines from Glasgow and Edinburgh converge before heading south to London. **Go through Carstairs village, past the coal-loading tower beside the railway, and then turn left to remain on the A70.** To the left of the road, near Corbiehall Farm, is the site of Castledykes Roman fort, whose earthworks are still visible.

At a T-junction near Hyndford Bridge, turn right onto the A73 towards Lanark. On the right is the old Lanark Racecourse, where the famous Silver Bells race was once run, and beyond is the entrance to Lanark Loch Country Park which offers boating, walking and a picnic area. The loch is a so-called 'kettle-hole' lake, a large depression in the underlying boulder clay created by a melting block of ice that was left in the wake of the last Ice Age. **Pass**

New Lanark

Lanark Auction Market on the right, then part of Lanark Grammar School on the left, before turning left on Braxfield Road, which leads downhill to New Lanark.

Return up Braxfield Road and turn left down the Wellgate. From the 'stop' sign at the bottom, take the road on the left on the far side of the church. As you leave Lanark, fork left on the A72 towards Hamilton. The road descends steeply towards the Clyde and the village of Kirkfieldbank. **At the foot of the hill, before the bridge, turn**

right at the sign for Clyde Valley Caravan Park B. The road crosses the Mouse Water, a tributary of the Clyde, which here issues from a narrow gorge. A much older bridge lies just upstream, while the main A73 road is carried high across the mouth of the gorge on the Cartland Brig, built 1822–23 by Thomas Telford. **At a gatehouse, fork left towards Nemphlar, and then go left again at a T-junction. When you reach the houses at Nemphlar turn right towards Crossford.** As the road descends again it affords a good view of the Clyde valley

---

• PLACES OF INTEREST •

New Lanark
The creation of David Dale and his son-in-law Robert Owen, the model village of New Lanark was the largest cotton-milling enterprise in early nineteenth-century Britain, and the focus for Owen's experiments in social reform. The River Clyde, which here flows swiftly through a narrow gorge, powered the huge waterwheels that drove the mill machinery, and over a thousand workers lived in the purpose-built tenements beside the factory buildings. It was a self-contained community run by a benevolent industrialist; Owen provided his workers with good accommodation, a contributory welfare system, free schooling, a cooperative store that sold low cost food, and a musical and dancing society. Miraculously, the village has survived almost intact

for over 200 years and is now preserved as a living museum. Some of the mill buildings contain exhibits on New Lanark's history, others house shops, a motor museum and a model railway, but most have been converted into flats and continue to provide accommodation for local people. Museums open daily 11–5. Telephone: (01555) 661345.

A short walk upstream from New Lanark leads to the Falls of Clyde, once one of the most impressive waterfalls in all of Britain. Unfortunately, since the gorge was dammed in 1926 for a hydroelectric power station, the falls have been reduced to a mere trickle, but once or twice a year, on special 'open' days, the sluices are opened and the cataract thunders again in all its former glory. The main fall, Corra Linn, is 80 feet (25m) high; a half mile

(0.8km) upstream, at the head of a narrow gorge, is the smaller Bonnington Linn, and above it the hydroelectric dam.

Falls of Clyde Visitor Centre, New Lanark. Scottish Wildlife Trust exhibition on local wildlife. Open Easter–late October, daily 11–5; October–Easter, weekends only 11–5. Telephone: (01555) 665262.

Craignethan Castle
Built in the sixteenth century on a picturesque promontory overlooking the River Nethan, this castle was probably the model for Tillietudlem Castle in Sir Walter Scott's novel *Old Mortality*. Open March–October, Monday–Saturday 9.30–6.30, Sundays 2–6.30; closed Thursday afternoons and Fridays in March and October. Telephone: (01555) 860364.

The River Clyde at New Lanark

ahead, which here is fairly straight with a flat floor and steep sides. This part of the Clyde has long been famous for its market gardens which produce most of Scotland's tomatoes, fruit, salad vegetables and bedding plants. **At the T-junction at the foot of the hill turn left.** On the left, just before the bridge, is the entrance to the Clyde Valley Country Estate which has a narrow-gauge railway, riverside walks, a gift shop and a garden centre. **Cross the bridge into Crossford and turn right onto the A72.**

At the end of the village pass the Tillietudlem Hotel and turn sharp left up a steep hill. By the houses at the top of the hill turn right towards Craignethan Castle C. As the road twists steeply down to the River Nethan, you can see the castle perched on its crag off to the right. **Turn right at the hamlet of Tillietudlem to visit Craignethan Castle.**

Continue into Blackwood, and turn left at a 'stop' sign onto the B7078. The prominent

summit of Black Hill, off to the left, is a famous viewpoint, commanding a panorama over the whole of the middle reaches of the Clyde Valley. **Continue straight through Kirkmuirhill, then cross the M74 motorway and go left at the roundabout. Exit left from the old dual carriageway into Lesmahagow.** This former coalmining village contains the excavated foundations of a Tironensian priory founded by David I in 1144. The excavations revealed part of a sophisticated plumbing system using lead and clay pipes. **Follow the main street through the village to a T-junction. Turn left, then right onto the dual carriageway, which is the B7078 (the old A74). About a mile beyond the Star Inn transport café turn left towards Douglas Water. The road crosses the M74 and after about 1¹/₂ miles, as it approaches the river, watch for a road on the right which leads across a wooden bridge to Douglas Water D.** The

lands around Douglas Water were the ancestral home of the powerful Douglas family. It was 'Good Sir James' Douglas, a commander under Robert the Bruce, who promised to carry his dead leader's heart to the Holy Land, but died during his crusade (the casket was returned to Scotland and was buried at Melrose Abbey). Sir James's tomb lies in St Bride's Church in the nearby village of Douglas. In the nineteenth and twentieth centuries the valley was a thriving coalmining community, but save for some open-cast workings the mines are now abandoned.

Go past the village, and where the road drops down to the right, fork left up the hill. Go straight on at the crossroads, on the B7055. The route now cuts across the moor to the west of Tinto Hill (2,334 feet, 707m), southern Lanarkshire's most prominent landmark. The hill is composed of a pale pink felsite rock which has proved more resistant to erosion than the surrounding sediments. It is a popular hill walk, and can be tackled steeply from nearby Wiston, or more easily from the north, near Thankerton. **Fork left E, still on the B7055, through the hamlet of Wiston. Where the road meets the A73 turn right, then first left towards Lamington. Turn left at the next T-junction onto the A702.** Here the route rejoins the River Clyde, and follows the line of the geological fault that separates the Southern Uplands from the Midland Valley, with good views of Tinto off to the left. **After 4 miles, where the road bends sharp left at Coulter Bridge, a right turn leads into the Culter Hills F.** You can drive into the hills as far as Birthwood Farm, where you must leave your car. This is the starting point for many good walks, including the ascent of Culter Fell (2,455 feet, 748m). **Continue on the A702 to return to Biggar.** ◼

Tinto Hill

MIDLOTHIAN: CRAIGMILLAR, ROSLIN, CRICHTON AND DUDDINGSTON

48 MILES – 2½ HOURS
START AND FINISH IN EDINBURGH

There are many quiet rural corners and fine, historic buildings within easy reach of Edinburgh. This tour takes in several of them, beginning with the fine castle of Craigmillar which actually lies within the city boundary, before visiting the architectural jewel of Rosslyn Chapel. Quiet back roads take you through peaceful countryside to the seemingly remote Crichton Castle, then back to the coast before returning by way of Duddingston village, a rustic gem that is almost in the heart of the city.

From the centre of Edinburgh, turn right at the east end of Princes Street, along North Bridge, South Bridge, Nicholson Street and Clerk Street. Turn left at the traffic lights at East Preston Street, then right along Dalkeith Road, following signs for Galashiels/Hawick/Jedburgh A7 (A68). Take the second exit at the big roundabout at Cameron Toll. As the road breasts the top of the hill, turn left on Craigmillar Castle Road **A** to visit Craigmillar Castle.

Return to the main road and turn left. The route passes a small group of houses called Little France, at the entrance to a caravan park. It was here, during the sixteenth century, that some of the French members of the court of Mary Queen of Scots lived. Continue out of Edinburgh on the A7 (A68) and go straight across at the ring road roundabout, taking the third exit into Dalkeith on the A68. Dalkeith stands on a ridge between the North and South Esk rivers, close to the point where the Roman road, Dere Street, once forded the stream. The town,

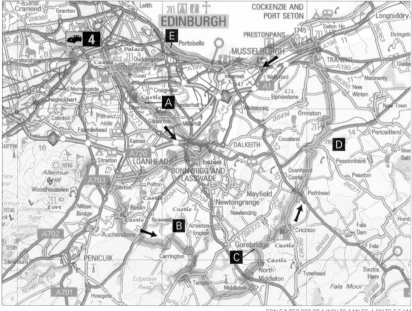

SCALE 1:250 000 OR 1 INCH TO 4 MILES 1 CM TO 2.5 KM

now a busy suburb of Edinburgh, grew up around Dalkeith House, the seat of the Earls of Morton and later the Buccleuchs. The grounds of Dalkeith House are open to the public, and have woodland walks, nature trails and a children's farm. **In Dalkeith, at the traffic lights at the top of the hill above Lugton Bridge, turn right towards Jedburgh, then go straight on at the next lights to a roundabout. Take the fourth exit, towards Lasswade and Loanhead, and go straight across at the next roundabout.** The road crosses the River North Esk and continues through the former mining town of Loanhead. In the eighteenth and nineteenth centuries the stretch of the river between Roslin and Dalkeith powered numerous mills and factories, including paper mills, barley mills, a gunpowder mill, brass and iron foundries, and a famous carpet factory. **Turn left onto the A701 (signposted Peebles) at a T-junction, then at the Bilston roundabout go left into Roslin. In the village the main road bends sharp right; go**

Craigmillar Castle

straight on here (called Chapel Loan) to visit the Rosslyn chapel and castle. There is a parking area beside the chapel from which you can walk downhill to the castle and Roslin Glen. The castle (not open to the public) is the ancestral home of the Sinclair family, Earls of Rosslyn, and suffered repeated burnings and sackings through its long history. A path leads steeply

down from the castle to the glen, where there are several riverside walks. Beside the path directly beneath the castle walls is an ancient yew tree, whose branches were once used to make bows.

Return to the main road and turn left, continue a short distance through the village, then turn left again (signposted Rosslynlee) and descend steeply into Roslin Glen. A right turn just before the bridge leads to a car park and picnic area near the site of the old gunpowder mill. Another car park beyond the bridge occupies the site of the old carpet factory. **As the road begins to climb away from the river, take the small road on the right towards Rosslynlee Hospital. At a T-junction turn left (signposted Carrington), and continue straight across the crossroads at the A6094. Soon after a sharp lefthand bend the route comes to a minor crossroads B with an inconspicuous sign for Carrington; turn right.** Carrington is a pretty little village in the middle of rolling farmland, built around a pink

---

• PLACES OF INTEREST •

Edinburgh
There are so many places to visit in Edinburgh that it is impossible to cover everything here. A section has been devoted to Edinburgh in the introduction (page 12). For further information on specific places of interest contact the Tourist Information Centre at Waverley Market, Princes Street. Telephone: (0131) 557 1700.

Craigmillar Castle
Craigmillar, one of Scotland's best preserved medieval castles, was a favourite residence of Mary Queen of Scots. She stayed as a guest of the castle's owner Sir Simon Preston, a provost of the city of Edinburgh, on two occasions: in 1563, when she received the ambassador of Queen Elizabeth I of England, and in 1566, following

the murder of her secretary Rizzio and the birth of her son, the future James VI. It was during this second visit that the earls of Argyll, Huntly and Bothwell, meeting at the castle, conspired to murder her husband, Lord Darnley. The castle is an impressive ruin with several interesting features, including a dungeon in which a skeleton was found in 1813.
Open April–September, Monday–Saturday 9.30–6.30, Sundays 2–6.30; October–March, Monday–Saturday 9.30–4.30, Sundays 2–4.30. Telephone: (0131) 661 4445.

Rosslyn Chapel
This little chapel, tucked away on the outskirts of Edinburgh, is one of Scotland's great masterpieces of the mason's art. It was founded in

1446 by William Sinclair, son of the Henry Sinclair who built the nearby castle, but it was never completed – what you see was intended to be the choir of a much larger church. The sculpted decoration of the interior is breathtaking in its intricacy and profusion – every column, capital, rib and lintel is encrusted with flowers, figures and foliage. The most famous feature is the 'Prentice Pillar', a column swathed with spiral wreaths, which is said to have been carved by an apprentice mason while his master was away. On his return, the master was overcome by jealousy of his pupil's skills, and killed him with a hammer. Open April–October, Monday–Saturday 10–5, Sundays 12–4.45. Telephone: (0131) 440 2159.

Rosslyn Chapel

sandstone church. **In the middle of Carrington village turn right towards Temple. At the next junction, bear right (away from a bridge) to reach Braidwood Farm. Turn left, through the farm, and pass through the steep-sided glen below the village of Temple.** This village is so named because during the thirteenth and fourteenth centuries the old, roofless church at the bottom of the glen was the Scottish seat of the ancient religious order known as the Knights Templar. Do not try to park here. Leave your car on one side or the other and walk

back down to see the chapel.

At the top of the hill on the far side, turn left, then right (away from the bridge). After half a mile turn right on a narrow road signposted Castleton/Esperston/Outerston. Bear right past Castleton Farm. The route now runs through an area of old limekilns and limestone quarries, which once produced agricultural lime for the region's farms. **Go left at the crossroads by Middleton Farm, then right at the lime works. Turn right on the main road (A7), then immediately left through North Middleton village and on past the entrance to Borthwick Castle Hotel.** Borthwick is one of the biggest and best preserved towerhouses in Scotland, built for Sir William Borthwick in the fifteenth century. It was visited by Mary Queen of Scots soon after her notorious marriage to Bothwell in 1567; pursued by her enemies, she was forced to escape disguised in men's clothing. The castle is now a hotel and is not open to the general public.

The road climbs up the far side of the valley to a little crossroads C marked only by a 'footpath' sign; turn right here. When the road forks, bear right. As you descend into

the next valley, the striking ruins of Crichton Castle come into view on the opposite hillside. **At the top of the hill on the far side of the valley, a road on the right leads to the car park for Crichton Castle. Immediately beyond is Crichton village, where the route turns left at the telephone box, towards Pathhead. In Pathhead turn right onto the A68, then first left, signposted Haddington. Turn right at a T-junction onto the A6093. One mile later, turn left D towards Ormiston.** The attractive village of Ormiston has a quiet, tree-lined

---

• PLACES OF INTEREST •

Crichton Castle
Although it looks grim and forbidding from the outside, the central courtyard of Crichton is one of the most delightful of any Scottish castle. The arcaded range on the south side, built 1581–91, is faced in diamond-faceted masonry in the style of the Italian Renaissance, no doubt inspired by the European travels of its owner Francis Stewart, the fifth Earl of Bothwell. Crichton Collegiate Church, by the parking area, was built in 1449 and has been in continuous use ever since. Open April–September, Monday–Saturday 9.30–6.30,

Sundays 2–6.30. Telephone: (01875) 320017.

Scottish Mining Museum
Exhibitions on East Lothian's coalmining industry, including steam locomotives, a steam crane, a colliery winding engine, and a beam engine of 1874. Open April–September, daily 11–4. Telephone: (0131) 663 7519.

Duddingston Village
This pretty little corner of Edinburgh, tucked beneath the slopes of Arthur's Seat, is best known for its church, whose fine Norman south door dates from the

early twelfth century. By the kirkyard gate is an octagonal watchtower, meant to deter body snatchers, and the 'Loupin-on Stane', a stone stair to help parishioners mount their horses after the service. Wrong-doers were chained to 'the Jougs', two iron manacles on the wall nearby. In the village street, called The Causeway, is the Sheep Heid Inn, named after the traditional Scots dish of sheep's head broth. It is one of Scotland's oldest taverns and is famous for the old skittle alley at the back. The loch beside the village is a nature reserve, and a favourite haunt of birdwatchers.

main street, with a stone Mercat
Cross dating from the fifteenth
century, one of the few surviving
crosses of that age in Scotland.
Continue into Tranent. The
mining town of Tranent bears the
distinction of having been one
terminus of Scotland's first ever
railway. Built in 1722, its
horsedrawn wagons carried coal
from the Tranent mines to ships
waiting at Cockenzie harbour, 2
miles away. **Go along the main
street, pass a pedestrian
crossing and turn right at a
mini-roundabout towards
Cockenzie. Go straight across
at the first roundabout
(junction with the A1), and
left at the second towards
Prestonpans.** A cairn to the left
of the road records the fact that it
was here, in 1745, that the
Jacobite army of Bonnie Prince
Charlie routed the government
forces of Sir John Cope.
According to one source, the
battle was all over in ten minutes,
with only 30 Highlanders dead but
over 400 government casualties.
    **Pass the railway station
and turn right into
Prestonpans. Turn right into
West Loan beside an old white
house with stepped gables.**
Here you can see Scotland's only
surviving example of an original,
early seventeenth-century Mercat
Cross, still occupying the site

where it was built. The white
house on the corner is Preston
Tower, a restored fifteenth-
century towerhouse with
seventeenth-century additions.
The house and its adjoining
period gardens are open to the
public. **Turn left at the T-
junction by the seafront.**
Prestonpans took its name from
nearby Preston ('priest's town')
which was owned by the monks of
Newbattle Abbey in Dalkeith, and
from the fact that here they heated
seawater in pans to make salt,
using the local coal for fuel. The
area's coalmining history is
recorded in the nearby Scottish
Mining Museum at Prestongrange.
    **At the roundabout by the
Levenhall Arms pub, go right
towards Edinburgh, and
along Musselburgh High
Street.** Situated on the site of a
Roman camp at the mouth of the
River Esk, Musselburgh has the
oldest racecourse in Scotland
(1816). The main road crosses
the river by the New Bridge (built
1806); upstream you can see the
Old Bridge (early sixteenth-
century). **Turn right across the
bridge over the River Esk at
the traffic lights. There is a
tourist information office in
the Brunton Theatre on the
right. The main road into
Edinburgh bears left at the
traffic lights, but the tour**

**goes straight on along the
Joppa seafront. At the traffic
lights in the middle of
Portobello (Bank of Scotland
on the far left corner) turn
left E along cobbled
Brighton Place and under a
railway bridge. Continue
along Duddingston Road,
straight across three sets of
traffic lights. Just past the
fourth set (a pedestrian
crossing), turn right down
Old Church Lane into
Duddingston Village.**
    **Go through the village and
into Holyrood Park. Turn left
at the roundabout to return to
Dalkeith Road. Turn right,
left, then right again to head
back to Princes Street.** ■

Crichton Castle

29

TWEED TO TALLA: PEEBLES, TRAQUAIR, ST MARY'S LOCH AND MEGGET

55 MILES – 2¹/₂ HOURS
START AND FINISH IN PEEBLES

The Tweed is one of Scotland's most beautiful rivers and nowhere is it more beautiful than the stretch between Tweedsmuir and Peebles. This tour cuts south from Peebles, deep into the Border hills to the lovely St Mary's Loch, then follows one of the loneliest roads in southern Scotland, climbing over the Megget Pass to Tweedsmuir, before following the valley of the Tweed back to Peebles. A long stretch of this tour is on a narrow, twisting road with steep gradients that reaches a height of 1,483 feet (452m), which is not recommended in winter.

Starting from the town of Peebles, cross the bridge over the Tweed and turn left on the B7062, following signs for Kailzie Gardens and Traquair House. At first the route follows the valley of the Tweed, Scotland's fourth longest river, and one of its most famous salmon fishing streams. It flows for 95 miles from its source at Tweed's Well (near the Devil's Beef Tub above Moffat) to Berwick-on-Tweed; for the last two miles of its course it lies entirely within England. **Two miles out of town on the left is the entrance to Kailzie Gardens.** These privately owned gardens put on a fine display at any time of year, from the snowdrops and crocuses of February and March to the reds and golds of autumnal trees. There is a walled garden and greenhouse, surrounded by 15 acres of wooded park, complete with duckpond. **Another 4¹/₂ miles leads to the entrance to Traquair House.**

From the Traquair House exit turn right along the B709 towards St Mary's Loch. The road passes through the tiny

Talla Reservoir

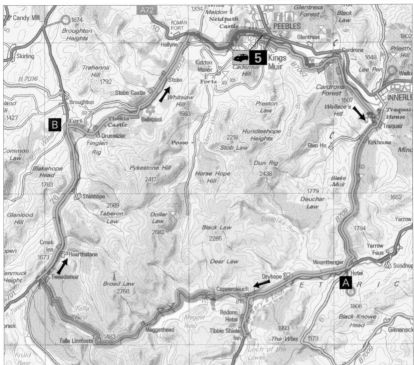

hamlet of Traquair before
climbing up the valley of the
Paddock Burn, which
unfortunately is gradually
disappearing beneath the spread
of forestry plantations. It crosses
the pass of Paddock Slack at a
height of 1,170 feet (357m), then
descends beside the Mountbenger
Burn, where James Hogg
(1770–1835), the poet and
novelist better known as 'the
Ettrick Shepherd', once had a
farm, before reaching the Yarrow
Water at the remote country hotel
called The Gordon Arms. **Turn
right on to the A708 at the
crossroads by the Gordon
Arms Hotel A.** The valley of the
Yarrow Water is broad and scenic,
surrounded by rounded, heather-
clad hills. As the ruffled waters of
St Mary's Loch come into view
ahead, you can see ruined
Dryhope Tower beyond the farm
to the right. This was the
birthplace of Marion Scott, 'The
Rose of Yarrow', who married
Auld Wat of Harden, one of whose
descendants was Sir Walter Scott
the novelist. **Pass the little kirk**

**at Cappercleuch, then turn
right towards Tweedsmuir.
Keep straight on at this
junction if you wish to visit
the Loch of the Lowes and
Tibbie Shiel's Inn.** St Mary's is
the largest natural loch in the
Borders, and also the most
beautiful. At its head, on a sandy
spit separating it from the smaller
Loch of the Lowes, stands the
early eighteenth-century hostelry
known as Tibbie Shiel's Inn.
Named after its first landlady, who
opened shop here in 1823 (and
died 55 years later at the grand
old age of 95), its guests included
such famous literary figures as
James Hogg, Sir Walter Scott and
Robert Louis Stevenson. There is a
small sandy beach beside the car
park, and on the hillside above it
a monument to 'the Ettrick
Shepherd'.

The road that runs from
Cappercleuch to Tweedsmuir is
one of the wildest and loveliest in
southern Scotland. It first hugs the
shore of the Megget Reservoir,
built in the 1980s and, along with
Talla and Fruid reservoirs, forms

part of Edinburgh's water supply.
There are several parking and
picnic areas along its banks, with
information boards detailing the
reservoir's construction and the
history of the valley. A few miles
further on the tour reaches its
highest point (1,483 feet, 452m)
at the Megget Stone, an old
boundary marker beside a cattle
grid. From this point, it is possible
to walk north to the rounded
summit of Broad Law (2,756 feet,
840m), a five-mile round trip that
should only be undertaken by
experienced and fully equipped
hill walkers. There is a parking
place a few hundred yards
beyond the cattle grid.

As the road descends towards
Tweedsmuir, you are rewarded
with superb views of Talla
Reservoir, hemmed in between
dark and craggy hills. It is the
oldest of Edinburgh's reservoirs,
built between 1895 and 1905; the
neat iron fence along its bank and
the trim masonry of the dam
contrast with the concrete and
boulders of the modern Megget
Reservoir. The road runs across

31

Peebles

Peebles is an attractive country town on the north bank of the Tweed, its broad High Street lined with shops and tearooms. It was a favourite hunting retreat of the early Scottish kings, but was frequently devastated by English invaders, and was occupied by Cromwell in 1650. Its oldest monument is the Cross Kirk, the ruined tower and nave of a thirteenth-century Trinitarian friary which was founded around a church said to house relics of the true cross. Other antiquities include St Andrew's tower, the mercat cross, and the five-arched Tweed Bridge which dates from the fifteenth century, though it has been widened twice since then. There are beautiful riverside walks along the banks of the Tweed in both directions, upstream to Neidpath Castle, and downstream to Kingsmeadow and Kailzie. Each year in June the town is taken over by Beltane week, a festival that combines an ancient Celtic fair with the Riding of the Marches. It culminates in a grand procession and the crowning of the Beltane Queen, on the Saturday nearest to Midsummer's Day.

Tweeddale Museum, High Street. The Chambers Institute, an eighteenth-century town house that was restored and gifted to the town by the publisher William Chambers in 1859, now houses a museum of local heritage and culture, including a gallery of contemporary art. Open Monday–Friday 10–1 and 2-5 (Easter–October only, weekends 2–5). Telephone: (01721) 720123.

Kailzie Gardens

Ornamental and wild gardens with plant centre, art gallery and restaurant. Open mid March–October, daily 11–5.30. Telephone: (01721) 720007.

---

the face of the dam then drops towards Tweedsmuir village, which has a pretty nineteenth-century church built of red

Talla Linns

sandstone. The kirkyard contains a memorial to John Hunter, a Covenanter who was murdered in 1685, and near to the gate another stone remembers more than 30 navvies who were killed during the construction of Talla Reservoir.

At Tweedsmuir the route crosses the River Tweed (here only a small stream), then turns right on the A701 towards Edinburgh. The route now follows the Tweed valley all the way back to Peebles. On the hillside above the road you can occasionally see the stumps of stone pillars that once supported the Talla Aqueduct, the pipeline that carried water from the reservoir to Edinburgh, a distance of 40 miles (see also Tour 10). You soon pass the Crook Inn, a coaching stage on the old road from Carlisle to Edinburgh that has been on this site since 1604. **Seven miles from Tweedsmuir, at Rachan Mill, turn right on the B712 (signs for Stobo and Dawyck Botanic Garden) B.** This road crosses the Tweed at a place called Merlindale, which recalls the legend that Merlin, King Arthur's mythical wizard, was buried where the Drumelzier Burn meets the Tweed. On the far side of the bridge is the hamlet of Drumelzier, and on the hillside beyond lies a crumbling heap of stone that was once Tinnis Castle. A few miles further on is the entrance to Dawyck Botanic Garden. The road crosses to the north bank of the Tweed and enters the hamlet of Stobo, whose venerable old kirk is said to stand on the site of an even more ancient church founded by St Kentigern in the sixth century.

At a T-junction turn right on the A72 back towards Peebles. The impressive Neidpath Castle soon comes into view on the right. **Go 250 yards past the castle and turn right into the car park.** Built in the late fourteenth century, with additions made in the seventeenth century, the castle occupies a dramatic position on a bluff overlooking the Tweed. Home successively to the Fraser, Hay and Douglas families, its many interesting rooms include a great hall with huge fireplaces, a pit prison (which is entered through a hole in the ceiling), and the Queen's Room, where Mary Queen of Scots is said to have stayed. The views from the parapets are excellent. A lovely walk leads along the riverbank into the town of Peebles. **Turn right out of the car park to return to Peebles.** ∎

Tweedsmuir Church

• PLACES OF INTEREST •

Traquair House
This grand old castle is the oldest continually inhabited house in Scotland. Though most of the building dates from the seventeenth century, the towerhouse in the northeast corner is much older. Still in the possession of the Stuart family, to whom it was gifted by James III in the fifteenth century, it is reckoned that no less than 27 Scottish and English monarchs have visited here. The house has a fascinating series of historic rooms, including secret passages and stairs within the walls. You might note as you arrive that the drive does not follow the grand tree-lined avenue in front of the house, but goes along one side of it. When Charles Edward Stuart left after visiting Traquair in 1745, the owner closed the gates behind the Bonnie Prince and swore that they would never be opened until a Stuart

monarch again sat on the throne. The Bear Gates, so-called because of the statues on the pillars, have remained shut ever since.

Attached to the house is the Traquair Brewery, which uses original eighteenth-century copper and wooden vessels to produce distinctive bottled and draught ales. There is also a lively annual fair, held here in early August.

Open Easter–September, daily 12.30–5.30 (from 10.30 July and August); October, Friday–Sunday 2–5. Telephone: (01896) 830323.

Dawyck Botanic Garden
These beautiful gardens, which cover a whole hillside, contain a large collection of trees and shrubs, with many fine, mature conifers and colourful rhododendrons. Planting was begun 300 years ago by the Vietch family, and continued under the Nasmyths and the Balfours, their

successors at Dawyck House. One of the larches was planted by the famous naturalist Carl Linnaeus in 1725. Many of the grand conifers in the garden were grown from seeds sent back from the western USA by the famous nineteenth-century botanist David Douglas (after whom the Douglas fir is named). The garden was gifted to the state in 1978, and planting continues today under the auspices of the Royal Botanic Garden in Edinburgh. A little chapel and kirkyard, containing the graves of the residents of Dawyck House, sit amid a stand of wild cherry trees in the middle of the grounds. Open mid March–late October, daily 10–6. Telephone: (01721) 760254.

Neidpath Castle
Open Easter–September, Monday–Saturday 11–5, Sundays 1–5. Telephone: (01721) 720333.

THE BORDER ABBEYS, THE WOOL TOWNS AND SCOTT COUNTRY

53 MILES – 2½ HOURS
START AND FINISH IN MELROSE

Set amid the Border landscape that so inspired Sir Walter Scott, this tour takes in the three great abbeys of Melrose, Dryburgh and Jedburgh, and the mill towns of Hawick and Selkirk, whose textile factories have converted the fleeces of Border sheep into fine woollen garments for over 150 years. The distinctive triple peaks of the Eildon Hills are a constant feature of the views along the way.

· PLACES OF INTEREST ·

Melrose
This historic town sits on the south bank of the River Tweed beneath the Eildon Hills, whose three summits inspired the name of the camp and signal station built here by the Romans: Trimontium or 'three hills'. It is best known for its beautiful Cistercian abbey, founded by King David I in 1136, and razed by English invaders in 1545. The abbey is one of Scotland's finest examples of Gothic architecture, and provided the inspiration for George Meikle Kemp, who designed Edinburgh's Scott Monument in the late 1830s. Beneath the east window you will find the last resting place of Robert the Bruce's heart, which was buried here after his friend Sir James Douglas died in an attempt to take it to the Holy Land. The enbalmed heart was found when excavations were carried out in 1920, and reburied.

Open April–September, Monday–Saturday 9.30–6.30, Sundays 2–6.30; October–March, Monday–Saturday 9.30–4.30, Sundays 2–4.30. Telephone: (01896) 822562.

Priorwood Garden, next to the abbey, specialises in growing plants for drying, and the NTS garden shop sells a wide range of dried flowers and pot pourri. There is an orchard too, with picnic tables. Open 1 April–24 December, Monday–Saturday 10–5.30, Sundays 1.30–5.30. Telephone: (01896) 822965.

Melrose Motor Museum. Collection of vintage cars, motorcycles and motoring accessories. Open Whit–October, daily 10.30–5.30. Telephone: (01896) 822624.

Dryburgh Abbey
The abbey was founded in 1150 and, like the other Border abbeys, was sacked by the English in the 1540s. Although little remains of the abbey church, the monastery buildings are well preserved, and enjoy a delightful wooded setting beside the Tweed. The graves of Sir Walter Scott and Field Marshal Earl Haig are in the north transept of the church.

Open April–September, Monday–Saturday 9.30–6.30, Sundays 2–6.30; October–March, Monday–Saturday 9.30–4.30, Sundays 2–4.30. Telephone: (01835) 822381.

From the car park at Melrose Abbey turn left past the abbey and the Motor Museum, on the B6361 through Newstead. Pass the disused Leaderfoot railway viaduct and turn left on the A68. The viaduct has 19 arches and stands 123 feet above the river, a monument to the skills of Victorian railway engineers. It was built in 1865, and remained in use for 100 years. Cross the new road bridge and take the first road on the right. At the foot of the hill go left towards Dryburgh. Take the second road on the right **A** signposted Dryburgh, to reach the parking area at Scott's View. Perched on the shoulder of a hill above a sweeping bend in the River Tweed, this was one of Sir Walter Scott's favourite spots. So accustomed were his horses to stopping here that when they finally drew his funeral carriage along this road towards Dryburgh Abbey, they paused at this point out of sheer habit. The view is a fine one of rolling fields and woods, dominated by the three heathery peaks of the Eildon Hills. About a mile further on is a smaller parking place, from which a five-minute walk leads to

Wallace's Statue, a huge red sandstone monument to the famous Scottish patriot. It was sculpted by a local mason and unveiled in 1814.

A mile and a half beyond Scott's View is a T-junction at the foot of a hill. Turn right here to visit Dryburgh Abbey, otherwise go left. At Clintmains turn right, then right again at the T-junction on the B6404 towards St Boswells. Pass through the village, and at the Buccleuch Arms Hotel turn left on the A68. Turn left again at the next junction, on the A699 to Maxton and Kelso. At the far end of Maxton village turn right towards Muirhouselaw and Fairnington. Rising ahead you can see the hill of Peniel Heugh, topped by the slender 150-foot tower of the Waterloo Monument. The tower was erected by the sixth Marquis of Lothian to commemorate the

Scott's View

Duke of Wellington's famous victory over Napoleon in 1815. Around it lie the earthwork remains of two prehistoric forts. **As the road begins to swing right beneath the monument, turn left down a narrow side road B. Turn right on the B6400 at the foot of the hill past the entrances to Monteviot House Gardens and**

Harestanes Woodland Visitor Centre. From the Visitor Centre (open April–October, daily 10–5), which has free parking, a wildlife garden, play area, craft shop and tearoom, a waymarked footpath leads to the summit of Peniel Heugh (a two-hour round trip). Another walk follows the line of Dere Street, the Roman road that runs from northern

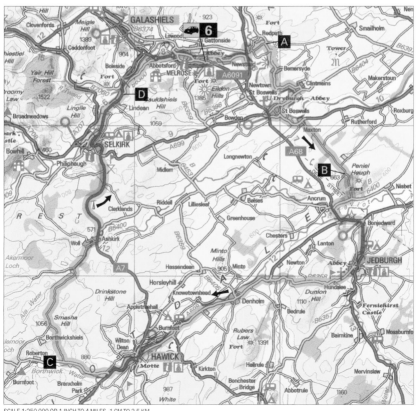

SCALE 1:250 000 OR 1 INCH TO 4 MILES *1 CM TO 2.5 KM*

Jedburgh

The old frontier post of Jedburgh, only 10 miles from the English border, is one of the region's most attractive towns. The impressive ruins of Jedburgh Abbey are the main attraction, but there are other historic buildings, and some good shops and tearooms. A self-guided tour leads you around the abbey, which was founded in 1138 and suffered the common Borders fate of repeated sackings by English raiders. The neighbouring visitor centre adds flesh to the historical bones. Open April–September, Monday–Saturday 9.30–6.30, Sundays 2–6.30; October–March, Monday–Saturday 9.30–4.30, Sundays 2–4.30. Telephone: (01835) 863925.

Mary Queen of Scots' House, Queen Street. The story of Scotland's tragic queen is told in this sixteenth-century house,

where Mary is said to have lodged in 1566. Open Easter–mid November, daily 10–5. Telephone: (01835) 863331.

Hawick

Known as the 'Auld Grey Toon', Hawick is the most important knitwear centre in the Borders. You can hunt for bargains in the town's many woollen shops and factory outlets, before taking a stroll along the wooded banks of the River Teviot. In Wilton Lodge Park on the western edge of town you will find the Hawick Museum and Art Gallery which details the development of the local knitwear industry, alongside exhibits on local history and wildlife. The surrounding park offers pleasant riverside walks and a scented garden set beside a little waterfall.

Hawick Museum and Art Gallery. Open April–September 10–12 and 1–5 (Sundays 2–5 only); October–March, Monday–Friday 1–4, Sundays 2–4, closed Saturdays. Telephone: (01450) 73457

Selkirk

A statue of Sir Walter Scott watches over the market place of the Royal and Ancient Burgh of Selkirk, outside the court room where he presided as Sheriff Depute of Selkirk County for 27 years. Set on a hillside above the Ettrick Water, the town was once famous for its 'souters' or shoemakers, but later made a living from its numerous woollen mills.

Halliwell's House Museum is housed in a row of eighteenth-century cottages on the main square and chronicles the town's history. Open April–October, Monday–Saturday 10–5, Sundays 2–4; July and August, daily 10–6; November and December, daily 2–4. Telephone: (01750) 20096.

Bowhill. Off the A708, 3 miles west of Selkirk. The nineteenth-century country seat of the Scotts of Buccleuch contains a magnificent collection of paintings, furniture and porcelain, while the grounds offer garden walks, nature trails, a riding centre, an adventure playground, gift shop and tearooms. House open 1–31 July, daily 1–4.30. Grounds open 1 May–August Bank Holiday, daily except Friday 12–5 (open Fridays in July, 1–4.30). Telephone: (01750) 20732.

Abbotsford House

Sir Walter Scott built this house as his country home, and today it is still owned by his descendants. Scott was an avid collector of historical relics and curiosities, and the house contains many fascinating items including Rob Roy's sword, a whisky glass used by Robert Burns, a lock of Bonnie Prince Charlie's hair, and a grisly portrait of the severed head of Mary Queen of Scots. Gardens and tearoom.

Open third Monday in March to 31 October, Monday–Saturday 10-5, Sundays 2-5. Telephone: (01896) 752043.

Jedburgh

England to Inveresk, east of Edinburgh. **Turn left on the A68 to Jedburgh.** The road crosses the River Teviot, then twists to the east to enter the lovely valley of the Jed Water. **In Jedburgh turn right at the signpost for Jedburgh Abbey, and then left into the car park beside the tourist information office.**

Turn left out of the car park, then left again at a T-junction, on the B6358 to Hawick. As you climb the hill out

of town you will pass Jedburgh Castle Jail Museum. The jail was built in the 1820s, on the original site of the town's castle, and is Scotland's only surviving example of a prison built to meet the requirements of the Howard penal reforms of the early nineteenth century. Period rooms and cells illustrate prison life, and a small exhibition covers the history of the town and castle.

As the road reaches the crest of the hill, you can see the Eildon Hills away to the north, and the nearer twin peaks of the Minto Hills. These and many other local hills are composed of intrusive igneous rocks, the resistant stumps of ancient volcanoes. **Four miles from Jedburgh bear left at the junction with the A698.** To the right of the road the tower of Fatlips Castle rears up from its wooded crag. Built in the 1850s on the site of an older castle, Fatlips once served as a showcase for the art collections of the Elliots of Minto. The route now heads up Teviotdale and through Denholm, whose village green is graced by an elaborate monument to Dr John Leyden. Leyden was born in 1755 in a thatched cottage on the far side of

the green, and became a famous linguist, mastering over 40 languages. Having trained as a minister and a doctor, he went to India and became Professor of Hindustani at Calcutta, but died of a fever in 1811. He was a poet and a friend of Sir Walter Scott, and collected much of the material for Scott's *Minstrelsy of the Scottish Borders*.

Soon the rooftops and chimneys of Hawick come into view ahead. **At the mini-roundabout in the centre of Hawick, go straight on towards Carlisle on the A7.** The busy High Street is lined with shops and is overlooked by the turreted Town Hall. On the way out of town you will see a lovely riverside green to your right. Here you will find the tourist information centre and the Hawick Museum and Art Gallery. **About 1 mile out of town turn right on the B711 to Roberton. After 2 miles the road dips and crosses over a small stream. Turn right immediately after the bridge C, along a road signposted to Harden and Borthwickshiels. This is a single track road with passing**

places, **so beware of sheep and lambs. At a T-junction by a tiny white cottage turn right.** The route now makes its way through grassy hilltops at around 1,000 feet above sea level, past flocks of sheep whose wool will end up in the knitwear shops of Hawick, Galashiels and other Border towns. As the road begins to drop into the valley of the Ale Water, there is a good view north to the Eildon Hills. **Five miles further on, turn left at Ashkirk on the A7 towards Selkirk.**

Follow the A7 through Selkirk and on towards Galashiels. After 2¹/₂ miles turn right on the B6360 to Abbotsford D. After about a mile or so the road dives into thick woods before passing the gatehouse to Abbotsford, the former home of Sir Walter Scott, which is now home to the writer's collection of curiosities. The car park for Abbotsford House is about 300 yards beyond the gatehouse. **At the roundabout beyond Abbotsford turn right on the A6091. At the next roundabout take the second exit to return to the starting point in Melrose.** ■

EAST LOTHIAN: HADDINGTON, EAST LINTON AND NORTH BERWICK

30 MILES – 1½ HOURS
START AND FINISH IN HADDINGTON

East Lothian is a region rich in both history and natural beauty, yet it lies only half an hour's drive from Edinburgh. This relatively short tour packs in a profusion of fascinating sights, and will take up most of a day if you try to see everything described here. The highlights are the impressive castles of Tantallon and Dirleton, the picture-postcard setting of Preston Mill and the lively resort of North Berwick.

Take the lefthand fork in Haddington's town centre (Market Street) and leave the town over the bridge at the traffic lights. As the road leaves town, you can see the ruins of the twelfth-century St Martin's Kirk across the football field on the right. East Lothian, which was once known as Haddingtonshire, has always been one of Scotland's most fertile areas: the county town of Haddington was, in the eighteenth and early nineteenth centuries, Scotland's leading grain market. The region also lay on the main invasion route from England into Scotland, and so has a rich legacy of defensive castles and fortresses. The first few miles of the route lead you through lush farmland on the right bank of the River Tyne, with the squat hump of Traprain Law (725 feet, 221m) ahead. The hill was the site of a prehistoric settlement, and from the first to the fifth centuries it may have been the capital of the

Votadini tribe, the native inhabitants encountered by the Romans during their invasion of Scotland in AD 83–84. Excavations carried out here in 1919 uncovered a famous hoard of Roman silver, which is now on

display in Edinburgh's Royal Museum of Scotland. The hoard, which dates from the fifth century, comprised bowls, cups, spoons, vases and wine jugs, many decorated with Christian symbols and motifs.

Three miles out of Haddington turn left on a narrow road which is signposted Hailes Castle A. About a mile from the junction is Hailes Castle (you can park in a lay-by just beyond the castle), beautifully situated on a rocky bluff overlooking the river. The castle is constructed around a central fortified manorhouse built for the Earl of Dunbar in the thirteenth century. It was extended with a curtain wall and square tower in the fourteenth and fifteenth centuries and incorporates two grim pit prisons, one beneath each tower, into which you can descend by ladder. The castle was visited by Mary Queen of Scots in 1567, during her flight with Bothwell to Dunbar. There are picnic tables overlooking the Tyne and a pleasant walk along the riverbank to East Linton. **Turn left at a T-junction a mile and a half beyond Hailes Castle. Go straight across the busy A1 road into East Linton. Pass under the railway bridge,**

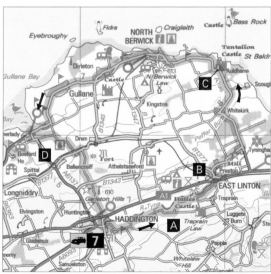

SCALE 1:250 000 OR 1 INCH TO 4 MILES *1 CM TO 2.5 KM*

turn left and then right (blue NTS signpost for Preston Mill).

Preston Mill

The road through the village crosses a sixteenth-century bridge over the River Tyne, to which East Linton largely owed its existence as a staging post on the Edinburgh–London road. It is an attractive village with a couple of good tearooms, and a fine example of thirteenth-century church architecture in the chancel of Prestonkirk, the parish church. **Pass the village green and go along the High Street for 200 yards. Turn right at Preston Road B onto the B1407 towards Preston Mill.** A short walk across the fields to the south of the mill leads to Phantassie Doocot, a sixteenth- to seventeenth-century building that once housed up to 544 nesting pigeons. The beehive-shaped structure is capped by a south-facing roof that provided a place for the birds to bask in the sun, and projecting courses of masonry were built to deter rats from climbing the walls and raiding the nests. Neighbouring Phantassie Farm was the birthplace of John Rennie

---

• PLACES OF INTEREST •

Haddington
For information see Tour 8.

Hailes Castle
Open at all times (no custodian). Telephone: (0131) 668 8800.

Preston Mill
This lovely old mill, with its sandstone walls and red pantile roofs, is one of the oldest working watermills in Scotland. The buildings date from the seventeenth century, and the machinery from the eighteenth, though grain has probably been milled on this site for at least 800 years. The mill remained in commercial use until 1957, when it was taken over by the National Trust for Scotland; it is now open to the public. The grain (mostly oats) was dried in the kiln, with its distinctive conical roof, before being ground between the stones on the upper floor of the mill building; shakers in the lower storey separated the husks from the meal.
Open Good Friday–30 September, Monday–Saturday 11–1 and 2–5.30, Sundays 1.30–5.30; October, weekends only 1.30–4. Telephone: (01620) 860426.

Tantallon Castle
The massive fortifications of Tantallon provide one of the most awe-inspiring sights in Scotland. A rocky promontory, surrounded on three sides by sheer cliffs dropping into the sea, is defended on the fourth by a huge, battlemented curtain wall of red sandstone. Built during the fourteenth century by the Earls of Douglas, and extended in the sixteenth century, it was deemed impregnable until advances in artillery allowed Cromwell's deputy, General Monk, to batter it into submission in 1651; the earthworks where the English guns were entrenched can still be seen. You can explore the pit prison and the many passages within the walls, and enjoy the magnificent views from the parapet.
Open April–September, Monday–Saturday 9.30–6.30, Sundays 2–6.30; October–March, Monday–Saturday 9.30–4.30, Sundays 2–4.30 (closed Thursday afternoons and Fridays in winter). Telephone: (01620) 892727.

North Berwick

This attractive Victorian seaside resort is a popular weekend destination for Edinburgh day-trippers who come to enjoy the sandy beaches, the open-air swimming pool, the golfcourses and the tearooms. On the rocky headland by the picturesque harbour lie the twelfth-century remains of the Auld Kirk, the site of a notorious witch trial in 1591 when several 'witches' were accused of conspiring with the devil to cause the death of James VI. The harbour is the departure point for boat trips around the Bass Rock. The prominent conical

hill of North Berwick Law (613 feet, 187m) rises to the south, capped by a whalebone arch and a watchtower manned in Napoleonic times to look out for the possible approach of a French fleet. The summit provides the finest viewpoint on this tour, offering a panorama over the Firth of Forth to the Isle of May and the Fife coast, and south to the distant Lammermuir Hills.

Dirleton Castle

The attractive wooded gardens that surround Dirleton Castle, complete with seventeenth-century bowling green and doocot, lend

the place a rustic air quite out of keeping with its original defensive purpose. The castle was built by the De Vaux family in the thirteenth century and originally consisted of three massive round towers connected by curtain walls. The stump of one tower remains, enclosing the impressive Lord's Hall, while the foundations of the others now lie beneath the fourteenth- and fifteenth-century range added by the Halyburtons, the De Vaux's successors. This incorporates a tiny chapel, beneath which is a cramped prison, which in turn overlies a horrific pit dungeon hewn from the solid rock.

Open April–September, Monday–Saturday 9.30–6.30, Sundays 2–6.30; October–March, Monday–Saturday 9.30–4.30, Sundays 2–4.30. Telephone: (01620) 850330.

Myreton Motor Museum

Open daily 10–6 (November–April, 10–5). Telephone: (01875) 870288.

(1761–1821), the renowned engineer whose many accomplishments included the construction of London Docks, the original Waterloo and London Bridges, and the Crinan Canal in Argyll.

Continue past the mill to Tyninghame village. Turn left at the T-junction onto the A198 towards North Berwick. This pretty little village of pink sandstone cottages was built in the nineteenth century to serve the needs of Tyninghame House, which stands to the east of the A198. The house is famous for its gardens which contain fine holly hedges, herbaceous borders, landscaped terraces and wooded avenues. Within the grounds lie the ruins of the twelfth-century St Baldred's Church, dedicated to an eighth-century anchorite who is said to have lived in a cave on the Bass Rock, and who is remembered in the names of two

rocks on the nearby coast – St Baldred's Boat and St Baldred's Cradle. The name Tyninghame is of Anglian derivation, meaning 'the farm on the Tyne', and indicates the great antiquity of the site: the Angles occupied Lothian between the seventh and the eleventh centuries.

About two miles after Tyninghame the route passes through Whitekirk, another historic village. In the fifteenth century this was a famous place of pilgrimage, with a healing well and a miraculous crucifix. It was visited in 1435 by a shipwrecked papal legate, who walked here from Dunbar to give thanks for his deliverance; he later became Pope Pius II. Hostels were built for the pilgrims, and also the fine fifteenth-century church of red sandstone which still stands beside the road. Behind the church is a sixteenth- to seventeenth-century tithe barn,

which was used by the monks of Holyrood Abbey (who owned lands hereabout) to store their 'tithe' – the one-tenth of the grain produced by local farmers that was given as a tax to support the church. The three-storey barn, with stepped gables and an outside staircase, was built with the stone from the old pilgrims' hostels.

Where the road bends sharp left at Auldhame Farm C, turn right to visit the beach at Seacliff. This private road (there is a fee payable for parking) leads in half a mile to a beautiful sandy beach with a fine view of the Bass Rock. This famous East Lothian landmark is a sheer-sided volcanic plug of basaltic rock rising 350 feet above the sea, and is home to Scotland's largest colony of gannets. It is topped by the ruins of a castle and a sixteenth-century chapel, reputedly built on the site of St

Baldred's cell. In the seventeenth century the rock was used as a prison for Covenanters and later for Jacobites, and Robert Louis Stevenson's fictional hero David Balfour was held captive here in the novel *Catriona*. Beyond Auldhame the massive pink sandstone curtain wall of Tantallon Castle comes into view on the right, with the guano-whitened bulk of the Bass Rock rising beyond. **Turn right at the entrance to Tantallon Castle car park.**

Return to the main road and turn right. The prominent cone of North Berwick Law rises ahead, while the islands of Craigleith, Lamb and Fidra lie in line off the coast to the right. Like Traprain Law and the Bass Rock, all of these craggy eminences are composed of intrusive igneous rocks, which are more resistant to weathering than the surrounding sediments. **At a roundabout turn right towards North Berwick, following signs into the town centre, where there are several car parks.**

Leave North Berwick along the High Street towards Edinburgh (A198). After 2 miles turn right into the village of Dirleton. Clustered around its triangular green and watched over by its venerable castle, Dirleton enjoys an enviable reputation as the prettiest village in Scotland. **Continue through Dirleton and rejoin the A198, turning right towards Gullane.** Pronounced 'Gillan', this tidy town is famous for its five golfcourses, one of which, Muirfield, regularly hosts the British Open Championship. It also has a good sandy beach. The road crosses the links beyond Gullane and reaches the shores of Aberlady Bay Nature Reserve, a wide expanse of sand and mud that shelters huge flocks of waders and seabirds. There is a car park and information board beside the mouth of the Peffer Burn, from which a footbridge leads to a path along the shore. Half a mile further on is Aberlady village, which was once the port for Haddington.

Bass Rock

Five miles beyond Dirleton, in Aberlady village, turn left on the A6137 towards Haddington. As the road leaves the village it bends sharp left then right, but at the second bend go straight on past Aberlady Mains Farm
D. At the next farm (Luffness Mains) turn right. A few hundred yards along this road is Myreton Motor Museum, which houses a varied collection of vintage cars, trucks, motorcycles and military vehicles. At a T-junction turn left onto the B1377 and after half a mile turn right towards Camptoun and Haddington. To the left of the road lie the extensive earthworks of The Chesters, one of Scotland's best-preserved examples of an Iron Age fort. There are two ramparts that completely encircle the fort, and a series of five earthworks which would have defended the western end. Within are traces of the foundations of over 20 circular stone buildings.

The final part of the route twists through the Garleton Hills, yet another outcrop of igneous rocks, capped by the pillar of the Hopetoun Monument, and offering a fine view over Haddington to the heathery flanks of the Southern Uplands. This road continues down the far side of the Garleton Hills and back into Haddington, the starting point.

Tantallon Castle

• TOUR 8 •

THE LAMMERMUIR HILLS, DUNS AND DUNBAR

66 MILES - 3 HOURS
START AND FINISH IN HADDINGTON

This route combines lonely hills and scenic coastline, striking southeast across the high moorland of the Lammermuir Hills to the Borders market town of Duns, then heading north through the secluded valley of the Whiteadder Water, before returning along the rocky shores of East Lothian to the fishing harbour of Dunbar. The final leg passes through the pretty villages of Stenton and Garvald. A long section of this route is on a minor road at over 1,300 feet above sea level which may be icy or even blocked by snow in the winter months.

Nungate Bridge, Haddington

Turn right at the east end of Haddington's main street. Immediately after crossing the bridge at the edge of town, turn left on the B6369 towards Lennoxlove and Gifford. On the right is the entrance to Lennoxlove House, the home of the Duke and Duchess of Hamilton. It was formerly called Lethington and was the seat of the Maitland family, one of whom was secretary to Mary Queen of Scots. It was renamed after the Duchess of Lennox (the model for Britannia on old British pennies) who bought the place in 1672. The Hamilton Palace collection of portraits, porcelain and furniture is on show. **In Gifford, turn left in front of the parish church on the B6355 to Duns.** The road begins to climb the scarp of the Lammermuir Hills. These are part of the Southern Uplands

which are separated from the Central Lowlands by a geological fault (marked by this scarp) which runs in a straight line from Dunbar on the east coast, to Girvan on the west. A lay-by near the top of the slope lets you stop to enjoy the view back north. From left to right you can see Arthur's Seat in Edinburgh, the tall chimney of Cockenzie power station, the low ridge of the Garleton Hills, conical North Berwick Law and the rounded hump of Traprain Law. Inchkeith and the Bass Rock lie offshore and on the far side of the Firth of Forth you may be able to see the twin peaks of the Lomond Hills in Fife.

Soon after reaching the crest of the hill, the road crosses a cattle grid and divides **A**. Take the righthand fork, signposted **Longformacus and Duns (15**

miles away). The route now traverses the rounded summits of the Lammermuir Hills, passing numerous starting points for easy hillwalks and a potential picnic spot where it crosses the Faseny Water. As you cross the shoulder of Cranshaws Hill, a fine view opens up of the twin humps of Dirrington Great and Little Laws, with the flat-topped bulk of The Cheviot on the horizon, before the road drops down to cross the Dye Water and the Southern Uplands Way at Longformacus. **At the T-junction with the A6105, turn left into Duns. As you enter the town, turn right along the High Street (signposted Town Centre) to the car park at the main square.**

At the junction beyond the square go left, then right on the A6112 towards Grantshouse. After 1 mile fork left towards Cranshaws and Gifford on the B6365. Three miles after the fork is a house on the left called Burnhouses **B**. Turn right here on a minor road to Abbey St Bathans. The road climbs steeply out of the valley. At the top you can see a trig point off to your right, surrounded by the earthworks of another hill fort. Just over 2 miles from

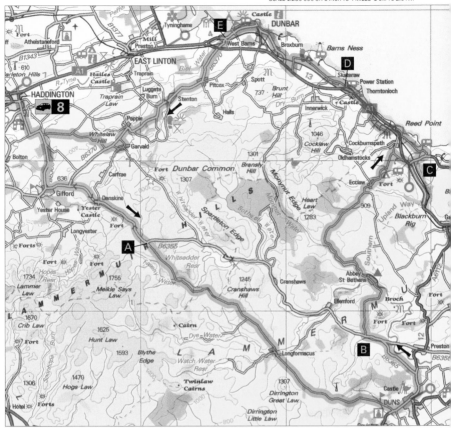

• PLACES OF INTEREST •

Haddington

The attractive county town of East Lothian was created a royal burgh in the twelfth century, and it still retains its medieval street plan. There are over 200 buildings of historical and architectural interest; a booklet called *A Walk Around Haddington*, available in local shops, guides you to the most interesting sights. The most impressive monument is the Collegiate Church of St Mary, dating from the fourteenth to fifteenth centuries. It resembles a cathedral in its large scale and grand design; the square tower was originally topped by an openwork crown spire like Edinburgh's St Giles. The church occupies a lovely wooded site beside the River Tyne, near the graceful arches of the sixteenth-century Nungate Bridge and the circular tower of Lady Kitty's Doocot. A gate leads from the churchyard into the garden of Haddington House, now known as St Mary's Pleasance. It has been restored as a typical seventeenth-century Scots garden with fruit trees, a boxed hornbeam walk, rose beds, a herb garden and a sunken garden.

The broad expanse of Court Street in the town centre is lined with elegant classical town houses which date from the eighteenth and nineteenth centuries. At the east end, where the street forks, is the the grand eighteenth-century Town House, designed by William Adam in 1748. A statue of John Knox, the famous Scottish church reformer, records the fact that he was born at nearby Mainshall Farm in 1505 and educated in Haddington's school.

In a close off High Street, to the right of the Town House, is the house where Jane Welsh Carlyle, wife of the nineteenth-century historian and philosopher Thomas Carlyle, was born. The house now contains a small museum of Carlyle memorabilia. Market Street, to the left of the Town House, leads to a bridge across the Tyne. The huge, red sandstone mill building here is one of several in Haddington, a monument to the town's industrial past. Across the bridge, to the right of the road, lies the ruined nave of St Martin's Kirk, a twelfth-century Romanesque building.

Lennoxlove House. Country house, with attractive gardens and tearoom. Open to the public April–September, Wednesdays, Saturdays and Sundays 2–5. Telephone (01620) 823159.

Cove Harbour

Burnhouses, where the road bends sharply left, there is a gate on the right and a signpost for the ruins of Edin's Hall Broch, one of the few Iron Age brochs in southern Scotland. If you want to visit it, continue to a riverside car park at the foot of the hill; the broch is a 1¹/₂ mile walk uphill from here.

Another half mile beyond the car park is the tiny hamlet of Abbey St Bathans with a youth hostel and a wooden suspension bridge that carries the Southern Uplands Way across the Whiteadder Water. The little church contains parts of the walls of a thirteenth-century church, and the tomb of a prioress. **At a junction 1 mile beyond Abbey St Bathans turn left towards**

• PLACES OF INTEREST •

Gifford
The village was built in the seventeenth and eighteenth centuries to house the people who worked in and around the estate of the nearby Yester House. Its picturesque main street, set off at the uphill end by a pretty parish church, offers a couple of good pubs and tearooms. The village was the birthplace in 1723 of the Reverend John Witherspoon, one of the signatories to the American Declaration of Independence.

Duns
A bronze statue in the town's public park claims this fine old Scottish burgh as the birthplace of the medieval philosopher John Duns Scotus (c.1266–1308). A more recent local hero is Jim Clark, the Motor Racing World Champion of 1962 and 1965 who was tragically killed on the racetrack at Hockenheim, Germany, in 1968. He is celebrated in the Jim Clark Memorial Trophy Room on Newtown Street. Duns Law (713 feet, 218m), a conical hill rising to the north of the town, is capped with the remains of earthwork fortifications occupied by the Covenanting Army of Sir Alexander Leslie in 1639. The view from the

summit (reached by a path on the southwest side) takes in the Lammermuir Hills to the north, and extends to Lindisfarne and the Cheviot Hills in the south.

Manderston House, about 2 miles east of Duns, is a grand Edwardian country house with beautiful gardens, a craft shop and

tearooms. Open May–September, Thursdays and Sundays 2–5.30. Telephone (01361) 883450.

Dunbar
The crumbling ruins of Dunbar Castle guard the narrow entrance to the town's pretty, rock-girt harbour, home to a dwindling fishing fleet and an RNLI lifeboat. The High Street contains two buildings of note: the Town Hall (which contains the tourist information office) dates from the seventeenth century, and the John Muir House museum. John Muir (1838–1914) emigrated to America at the age of 11, and became an influential naturalist and writer who helped to create the USA's national parks system. John Muir Country Park, to the west of town, offers good coastal walks and birdwatching.

John Muir House. Open June–September daily, except Wednesday and Sunday, 10–12.30 and 1.30–4.30. Telephone: (01368) 863353.

Torness Nuclear Power Station Visitor Centre open daily 9.30–4.30. Guided tours begin at 9.45, 11.15, 1.30 and 3. Telephone: 0800 250255.

Bushelhill and Monynut. The route now winds along the upper reaches of the narrow Whiteadder valley, with sheep and cattle wandering nonchalantly across the single-track road: drive slowly and take especial care during the lambing season. The road finally climbs out of the valley and breasts a rise, revealing a view of the North Sea.

After about 5 miles turn left at a T-junction just after a cattle grid. At another T-junction, 2 miles later, turn right (on the old A1) to reach the new dual carriageway. Turn right, cross a bridge, and take the first exit on the left, the A1107 towards Coldingham. The road crosses the railway, then a deep wooded valley (Pease Dean Wildlife Reserve). **Two hundred yards later take the narrow road on the left** **C** **leading to Pease Bay.** The road bends sharp left with a view of Torness Nuclear Power Station and the Bass Rock ahead, before dropping steeply down to the sandy cove of Pease Bay, which has a large caravan park and a good sandy beach.

The road fords a stream then climbs away from the bay and becomes two-lane. Turn right here to visit Cove Harbour. The side road ends at a public parking area which is the starting point of the Southern Uplands Way long distance footpath. Beyond the car park a wooden staircase and footpath lead down through a tunnel to picturesque Cove Harbour. **At the roundabout on the A1 go straight across (signposted Cockburnspath), and turn immediately right to Dunglass.** Just after crossing a stone bridge over a deep gorge, you will see the entrance to Dunglass House. In the grounds is Dunglass Collegiate Church, a handsome fifteenth-century building with stone-slab roof, containing the family tombs of the founder, Sir Alexander Hume. **Beyond Dunglass the road**

Barns Ness lighthouse

joins the A1. Go past the entrance to Torness Power Station Visitor Centre and just after the dual carriageway ends turn right towards Skateraw **D**. There are some good beaches and picnic sites off this road. You can park at Skateraw, Barns Ness and White Sands. Barns Ness Lighthouse, 120 feet tall, is an important landmark for coastal shipping. On a clear day you can see the low outline of the Isle of May, 14 miles to the north.

The road returns to the A1. Turn right for half a mile, then take the first exit right on the A1087 towards Dunbar. Yet another right turn takes you into Dunbar. The village of Broxburn, at the Dunbar turning, lies near the site of the famous Battle of Dunbar (1650), when Cromwell's troops inflicted a humiliating defeat on the Covenanting army of Sir Alexander Leslie. Dunbar itself is a pleasant harbour town with good pubs and enjoyable coastal walks. **Leave Dunbar on the Edinburgh road. As you enter the village of West Barns** **E** **turn left on the B6370 just after the first bus stop, towards Stenton and Garvald (the signpost is hidden by**

trees on the righthand side of the road). **At the A1 turn right and immediately left to remain on the B6370.** This scenic road (part of the East Lothian Hillfoot Trail) runs along the northern edge of the Lammermuir Hills, passing through a couple of quiet and attractive villages. To the right of the road, as you enter Stenton, is a conical structure that houses an ancient pilgrim's well. The village green has a Wool Stane, or tron, used for weighing wool at market time, and an old dovecot with crow-stepped gables. **Just beyond Stenton, turn left towards Garvald and Gifford. After 3 miles turn left on the very narrow road that leads to Garvald.** This tiny village has a single narrow street lined with red sandstone cottages, and a pub called the Garvald Hotel. A bridge over the stream leads to Nunraw, a sixteenth-century towerhouse belonging to the modern Cistercian convent of Nunraw Abbey, which lies further uphill. **Continue through Garvald, and turn left at the T-junction beyond the village. Take the first road on the right, which leads back to the B6369 and so to Haddington.** ■

ST ANDREWS AND CUPAR VIA THE EAST NEUK OF FIFE

46 MILES – 2 HOURS
START AND FINISH IN ST ANDREWS

The eastern part of Fife contains some of central Scotland's most attractive scenery and a fine collection of historic towns. St Andrews was the ecclesiastical capital of Scotland for many centuries, and the site of the country's first university. The tour starts here then heads south and west along the East Neuk, a stretch of scenic coast dotted with picturesque villages, to the sandy shores of Largo Bay, home of the original Robinson Crusoe. The return journey takes in the country house at Hill of Tarvit and the old county town of Cupar.

In St Andrews drive east along South Street (towards the cathedral) and turn right at the end, on the A917 to Crail. The road climbs away from the town through lush farmland. The hamlet of Boarhills, 4 miles from St Andrews, is said to take its name from an ancient swine-worshipping cult that was centred here before the arrival of Christianity. **About 2 miles further on, at Kingsbarns, take the second street on the left after the post office A to visit the beach at Cambo Sands.** This pleasant sandy beach sits alongside a tiny, man-made boat haven for local lobster fishermen. **Return to the main road and go left. As the route enters Crail, the main road bends sharp right in front of the Golf Hotel. Turn left here for the parking area beside the tourist information office.**

The town of Crail received its royal charter in 1178, making it one of the oldest royal burghs in Scotland. The tourist office is housed in the sixteenth-century Tolbooth, near to the Mercat Cross, which is topped by a stone unicorn, symbol of the Scottish

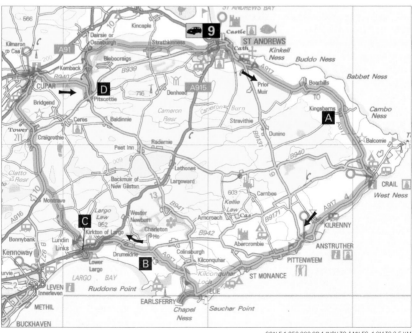

SCALE 1:250 000 OR 1 INCH TO 4 MILES *1 CM TO 2.5 KM*

St Andrews

The origin of St Andrews is lost in the mists of time, but it is a very ancient settlement indeed. Legend has it that, in the fourth century AD, St Rule took charge of the holy relics of St Andrew (brother of St Peter) who had been crucified on a diagonal cross in Patras, Greece. He had been told to take them to a land far in the west, 'in the utmost part of the world', and while sailing through the North Sea was shipwrecked on the coast of Fife, near the Pictish settlement of Kinrimund. The local Celtic church took on a new importance (and a new name – St Andrews) with the possession of such important relics, and in 908 it became Scotland's only bishopric and a place of pilgrimage. In the twelfth century the country's biggest cathedral was begun, and in 1412 its first university was founded here. The town escaped industrialisation in the nineteenth and twentieth centuries, and today it retains a scholarly and ecclesiastical air.

Since the mid-nineteenth century St Andrews has attracted a different kind of pilgrim, but no less fervent in his devotions than the early monks. Thousands of golfers come each year to pay their respects at The Royal and Ancient Golf Club and, if possible, to play a round or two on the world-famous Old Course.

St Andrews Castle, though now in ruins, occupies a fine clifftop site. You can explore a tunnel dug beneath the walls during a sixteenth-century siege, a unique survival of a 'mine and countermine'. There is a visitor centre. Open April–September, Monday–Saturday 9.30–6.30, Sundays 2–6.30; October–March, Monday–Saturday 9.30–4.30, Sundays 2–4.30. Telephone: (01334) 477196.

St Andrews Cathedral, once the largest religious building in the country, stands in atmospheric ruin on one of Scotland's holiest sites. Near the twelfth-century east end stands the older tower of St Rule's Church (c.1130) which offers a fine panorama over the town. On the clifftop outside the kirkyard walls are the foundations of the even older Church of the Blessed Mary on the Rock, dating from the ninth to the tenth centuries, which once held the relics of St Andrew. Cathedral and museum open same times as castle. Telephone: (01334) 472563.

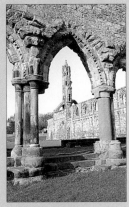

Crail Museum and Heritage Centre. Tourist Information Centre, 62–64 Marketgate. Exhibition illustrating the history of the town. Open Easter, and June–mid September, Monday–Saturday 10–12.30 and 2.30–5, Sundays 2.30–5. Mid September–May, weekends only, 2.30–5.

monarchy. The town originally made a living from fishing and trade with the Low Countries whose influence can be seen in the crow-stepped gables of the houses and their red pantile roofs; the tiles were brought back from Holland as ballast in empty cargo vessels. If you drive out of town past the Tolbooth, you come in about 2 miles to a car park at Fife Ness, a rocky headland capped by a lighthouse and a coastguard station with a golfcourse in its lee. There are good clifftop walks here. **Return to the main road and continue on the A917 through Crail towards Anstruther, 3½ miles away.** The 10-mile stretch of rocky coast between Fife Ness and Largo Bay is known as the East Neuk of Fife (*neuk* is Scots for 'corner' or 'promontory'), and is famous for its picturesque fishing villages.

The route continues along the A917 through Pittenweem, St Monance and Elie. Pittenweem is still a busy fishing port, and in bad weather the harbour can be chock-a-block with boats. In Cove Wynd, a steep alley behind the quayside, is St Fillan's Cave, the retreat of a seventh-century Irish missionary, which gave the town its name (pittenweem means 'place of the cave' in the Pictish tongue). Above the cave are the remains of a priory established in the twelfth century. Another early Irish saint, St Monan, gave his name to St Monance, when his relics were brought here by Irish missionaries attempting to escape Viking attacks. The ancient Church of St Monan was built by David II in 1362 in gratitude for the healing of his arrow wounds through prayer at the shrine, but it stands on an even older site associated with fourth-century St Ninian. It is a true fisherman's church, lashed by salt spray, and containing many nautical motifs, including a model of a fully rigged ship made in 1800.

Elie and its neighbour Earlsferry stand on a beautiful sandy bay. For hundreds of years ferries plied the waters between here and North Berwick, but now both towns earn their living as holiday resorts. Elie is the starting point for a lovely walk along the coast to St Monance. **In the middle of Elie the main road bends sharp right at the church; go straight on to visit Earlsferry, otherwise continue on the A917 towards**

Mercat Cross, Crail

Crail

Leven. Turn left at 'give way' sign **B**. Ahead rises the conical peak of Largo Law (952 feet, 290m) on whose slopes there was once a prehistoric settlement. Local legend claims that a tinker found a hoard of silver here in 1819 and later excavations unearthed a fine collection of silver vessels and jewellery, some bearing Pictish symbols, which are now housed in Edinburgh's Royal Museum of Scotland.

Go through Upper Largo, then turn left off the A917 past the petrol station to visit Lower Largo (limited parking). The road winds downhill and passes under a bridge to arrive at a hotel beside a tiny harbour. **At the foot of the hill, beside the river mouth, go left to find a parking area.** About a hundred yards further along you will find the Robinson Crusoe statue, set in a niche above the doorway in a pink sandstone cottage. The statue commemorates Alexander Selkirk, who was born in a house on this site in 1676, and whose desert island adventures inspired Daniel Defoe to write his famous story of Robinson Crusoe. **Return to the river mouth and go straight on across the bridge.**

Follow the road through the village to a T-junction and turn right, back onto the A917. Pass the Lundin Links Hotel, cross a small bridge, and turn left (signposted Cupar) C. After about 3 miles, at the T-junction with the A916, turn right towards Cupar. The route now passes through the village of Craigrothie, an old coaching stop on the road to Cupar and St Andrews, with a fine eighteenth-century inn. **At the top of the hill turn right into the entrance to Hill of Tarvit Mansionhouse.** Once you have seen the mansionhouse and gardens, you can ask for the keys to Scotstarvit Tower, a fifteenth- to sixteenth-century towerhouse about 10 minutes walk away on the other side of the main road. The L-shaped tower, with only a few tiny windows, is in excellent condition.

The road descends the far side of the hill and joins the A92. There is a good view off to the left here over the Howe of Fife, a basin of fertile farmland overlooked by steep hills of resistant volcanic rock. Across the valley to the north is wooded

St Monance

Anstruther

This former fishing community can boast the longest official name in Scotland – the United Burghs of Kilrenny, Anstruther Easter and Anstruther Wester – but the locals call it simply 'Enster'. Until the collapse of the herring industry in the 1930s this was one of the main centres of Scotland's herring fleet and it was also an important trading port.

From May to September there are daily boat trips from the harbour to the Isle of May, about 5 miles offshore. The island is a nature reserve where you can see grey seals and huge breeding colonies of seabirds including puffins, razorbills, kittiwakes and guillemots.

Scottish Fisheries Museum. A fascinating collection of ships' gear, fishing equipment and model boats tells the story of the local

fishing industry. The museum's pride and joy is the Reaper, a traditional nineteenth-century fishing boat that has been restored and is now on display in the harbour. There is also a marine aquarium. Gift shop and tearoom. Open April–October,

Monday–Saturday 10–5.30, Sundays 11–5; November–March, Monday–Saturday 10–4.30, Sundays 2–4.30. Telephone: (01333) 310628.

Hill of Tarvit Mansionhouse and Garden

This fine Edwardian country house was built in 1906 for Mr F. B. Sharp, a Dundee industrialist, and was bequeathed to the NTS in 1949. The house is now open to the public, displaying Mr Sharp's collections of fine French furniture, Chinese porcelain and paintings by Raeburn and Ramsay. The lovely gardens contain a restored Edwardian laundry, and occasionally host weekend sales of garden plants. House open Good Friday–late October, daily 1.30–5.30. Garden and grounds open all year, daily 9.30–sunset. Telephone: (01334) 653127.

Mount Hill, topped by the obelisk of the Hopetoun Monument, erected in 1827 in memory of the fourth Earl of Hopetoun. **Turn right into Cupar. Cross the railway bridge and turn right along Station Road to a car park outside the tourist information office.** Cupar was the county town of Fife, and one of its main commercial centres. Its past prosperity is manifested in its many fine Georgian and Victorian buildings, notably the Corn Exchange tower. **Turn right out of the car park and turn right at the junction with Pitscottie Road. Follow this road, the**

B940, to the village of Pitscottie. Opposite a service station, and just before the crossroads, turn sharp left towards Kemback and Dairsie **D**. The route now heads down the narrow, wooded gorge of Dura Den. The waters of the Ceres Burn, which runs through the Den, once powered a number of flax mills, whose ruins lie along the course of the stream. Many of the workers' cottages and old mill buildings have been restored as houses and flats.

At a T-junction by a narrow bridge, turn right. The road climbs slowly up onto the crest of a ridge, with magnificent views to the north across the Eden estuary and the Tay to the distant Highlands, while ahead you can see the spires of St Andrews on the horizon. **Go straight across the crossroads at Strathkinness. At a 'give way' sign in the suburbs, turn left onto the B939 to arrive at the West Gate of St Andrews, and so back into South Street, returning to the starting point of the tour.** ■

THE PENTLANDS, WEST LINTON, GLADHOUSE RESERVOIR AND NEWTONGRANGE

52 MILES – 2½ HOURS
START AND FINISH IN EDINBURGH

One of Edinburgh's great attractions is the ease with which it possible to escape to the hills. The Pentlands immediately to the south, and the Moorfoots a little further off, have long provided a tramping ground for weary city dwellers. This tour runs along the southern flank of the Pentlands, passing through the pretty villages of Carlops and West Linton, then strikes out towards the Moorfoots and the attractive manmade loch of Gladhouse Reservoir. It also offers the chance to study two of the region's traditional industries: glassmaking at Penicuik, and coalmining at Newtongrange. The tour takes in some lovely scenery, but there are also many indoor attractions, making it a good choice for a rainy day.

At the east end of Princes Street in central Edinburgh, turn right along North Bridge, and after about a mile turn right at the traffic lights at Hope Park Terrace, then left at the next lights onto Causewayside. One mile later, at the traffic lights on Mayfield Road, at Kings Buildings, turn right along West Mains Road. Beyond

Kings Buildings, a red sandstone arch on the left marks the entrance to Blackford Hill. You can drive to a car park on the summit of Blackford Hill, which is one of the finest viewpoints in the city. Looking to the north, over the sprawling Victorian suburbs of Marchmont and Grange, you can see the jagged ridge of the Old Town stretching between the

castle crag and Arthur's Seat. To the south lie the Braid Hills, with the heathery slopes of the Pentlands in the background. Beside the car park is the Royal Observatory, built in the 1890s, and now open to the public. Footpaths on the south side of the hill lead down to the Hermitage of Braid, an attractive wooded glen with a nature trail and wildlife centre. Beside the quarry to the east of the glen is Agassiz Rock, named after a Swiss geologist who visited Edinburgh in 1840. On examining this outcrop, which is covered in deep gouges, Agassiz declared that the marks were caused by a glacier, the first time that the effects of glaciation had been recognised in Scotland.

Continue on West Mains Road, and bear left at the traffic lights along Charterhall Road and then Cluny Gardens. At a T-junction and traffic lights at

The Royal Observatory at Blackford Hill

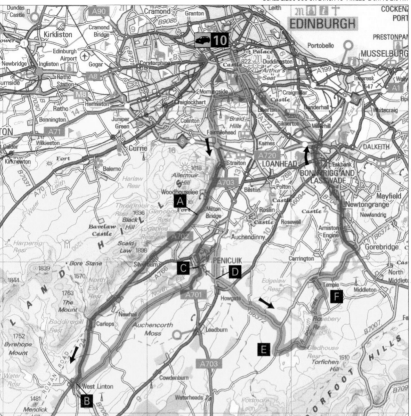

the Hermitage Bar turn left on Braid Road. Follow it up the hill and straight across a mini-roundabout until it joins Comiston Road. The road passes the Braid Hills Hotel, whose tearoom was the setting for a crucial confession in Muriel Spark's famous novel *The Prime of Miss Jean Brodie*. **Follow Comiston Road and its continuation out of the city towards Penicuik and Biggar, crossing the ring road at the Fairmilehead Inn.** As the route heads out of the city, the bluff northern slopes of the Pentland Hills rise to the right, home to Europe's largest dry ski slope. The Hillend Ski Centre has been in operation since 1964, and has two main runs of 400 yards each, complete with chairlift. The centre's car park is also a popular starting point for walks in the northern Pentlands. Swanston village, less than half a mile away

across the golfcourse, was a childhood haunt of the novelist Robert Louis Stevenson. Its thatched and whitewashed cottages are picturesquely arranged about a village green at the foot of the hills.

Where the road forks beyond Hillend, bear right on the A702 towards Biggar. After 2½ miles turn right at the Flotterstone Inn to visit the Pentland Hills Visitor Centre A. This valley is the main route into the heart of the northern Pentlands, which provide a welcome escape for nearby city dwellers. The visitor centre houses a display on local wildlife and dispenses maps and advice on exploring the hills. Several excellent walks begin here, either along the valley to Glencorse Reservoir or up onto the summit ridges. About half a mile to the north of Flotterstone is Castlelaw Hill Fort, a 2,000 year

old Iron Age fort with a souterrain (underground storage chamber) built into the ramparts The hill above is an army firing range; do not enter when the red flag is flying. To the southwest of the centre is Rullion Green, the site in 1666 of a battle between a band of Covenanters and a government force led by Sir Thomas Dalyell. The Covenanters were defeated and those taken prisoner were either hanged or deported to Barbados. The event is commemorated by the Martyrs' Tomb, hidden in the trees above the green.

Return to the main road and continue towards Biggar. The road hugs the foot of the hills, which extend to the southwest as far as Carnwath, roughly following the line of a Roman road. At Silverburn you pass beneath Scald Law, at 1,898 feet (579m) the highest summit in the Pentlands. The little village of Carlops, a few

51

Royal Observatory

Built in the 1890s to replace the older observatory on Calton Hill (whose view had been eclipsed by the smoke billowing from neighbouring Waverley Station), the Royal Observatory played an important part in the development of astronomy in Scotland. It now houses a visitor centre with exhibitions on space research and cosmology. Open April–September, daily 12–5.30; October–March, Saturday–Thursday 1–5, Fridays 1–9. Telephone: (0131) 668 8405.

West Linton

Lying at the southeastern end of the Cauldstane Slap, an important track across the hills, West Linton was once a tollgate on the drove road between the Borders and central Scotland. The old tollhouse still exists beside the village green, near to the parish

kirk, whose graveyard contains a fine selection of ancient headstones decorated with skulls,

bones and winged hour glasses. The village clock sits on the site of Lady Gifford Well which has lain unused since Victorian times. On the front of the clock is a statue of Lady Gifford, carved in 1666; the house opposite bears a panel showing James Gifford with his eldest son and six of his ancestors. The village can also boast a couple of pubs, an excellent tearoom and a secondhand bookshop.

Edinburgh Crystal Visitor Centre

Edinburgh has had a glassmaking industry for at least three centuries, and one of its oldest firms now runs this factory in Penicuik. The visitor centre explains the history of glassmaking, and the factory tours (available all year, Monday–Friday 9.15–3.30, and 11–3 on Sundays in May–September) lead you through the process of mixing, blowing, moulding, cutting and engraving.

Open Monday–Saturday 9–5, Sundays 11–5. Telephone: (01968) 675128.

Lady Victoria Colliery

This mine has been preserved as a working museum of the Scottish coal industry. Guided tours take you around the pithead equipment, which includes a huge steam winding engine, and there are exhibits describing the history of the mine, the daily lives of nineteenth-century miners, and the trades they practised. Open March–October, daily 10–4 (last tour at 3). Telephone: (0131) 663 7519.

stone tower, and a couple of stone pillars, apparently serving no purpose. These once supported the Talla Aqueduct, a nineteenth-century pipeline that carried drinking water from Talla Reservoir (see Tour 5) to Edinburgh, a distance of nearly 40 miles.

After 7 miles turn left at a T-junction, on the A701 towards Penicuik. (To avoid Penicuik, turn right on the B6372 to Gorebridge before the bridge at the foot of the hill C. This takes you to the staggered junction mentioned at D below.) Penicuik was originally a papermill town, but it is now a busy suburb of Edinburgh which has clearly moved with the times – history has left few relics here. The Edinburgh Crystal factory is the biggest attraction. **Follow the main road through Penicuik. Pass two service stations on the right, then turn right, on a road signposted for Edinburgh Crystal Visitor Centre.**

Continue past the Edinburgh Crystal works and through a housing estate. Turn left at a T-junction, then

miles further along, has survived almost intact for 200 years. The village pub, the Allan Ramsay, is named after the eighteenth-century poet whose best known work, *The Gentle Shepherd*, is set in the environs of Carlops. Many of the local place names – Habbie's Howe, Peggy's Lea and Patie's Hill, for example – are taken from *The Gentle Shepherd*. **At West Linton, 9 miles after the Flotterstone Inn, turn left**

towards the village centre.

Leave West Linton on Deanfoot Road B, opposite the Linton Hotel. This minor road leads across the bleak expanse of Auchencorth Moss and provides a superb panoramic viewpoint from which to admire the long ridge of the Pentland Hills with the conical peaks of East and West Kip prominent to the left of Scald Law. To the left of the road you will see a square

left again. The road heads downhill to the River North Esk. **Cross the bridge and turn sharp left. At the T-junction at the top of the hill, turn right onto the B7026. At a staggered junction turn left, onto the B6372 D then continue straight across a crossroads towards Gorebridge.** The route now strikes out across rolling farmland towards the rounded forms of the Moorfoot Hills. **Three miles later the road bends sharp left, but turn right towards Gladhouse. When the road enters a forestry plantation look out for a small road on the left, also signposted Gladhouse**

E. This little road runs along the northern edge of Gladhouse Reservoir, one of the many that supply water to Edinburgh. It is a popular trout-fishing loch and there are a number of appealing picnic spots around its banks which are lined with Scots pines and wild roses. Beyond the dam there is a car park with an official picnic area. It is possible to follow a footpath from the east side of the loch up to the crest of the Moorfoot Hills which offer a grand view north to the Pentlands.

Turn left at the T-junction beyond the dam. After a mile or so this road joins another coming from the right, then climbs over a hill and down to a T-junction F. Turn left

here into the village of Temple. This remote spot was once the seat of the Knights Templar in Scotland, but all that remains is a ruined fourteenth- to fifteenth-century church in the glen below the village. **Turn right onto the B6372 at the junction by the bridge at the foot of the hill. Turn left at a crossroads with the A7. Two miles further on the road passes beneath the walkway at the Scottish Mining Museum in Newtongrange.** The earliest records of coalmining in Scotland show that in the thirteenth century the monks of Newbattle Abbey at nearby Dalkeith used local coal to make salt by heating seawater. By the nineteenth and twentieth centuries the Midlothian coalfield was one of the country's biggest producers. Miners at the Lady Victoria Colliery in Newtongrange dug out over 40 million tons of coal during its 90 years of productive life, but following the closure of the mine the local communities of Gorebridge and Newtongrange have had to look elsewhere for employment. **Follow the A7 back into the centre of Edinburgh.** ■

Flotterstone Inn

STIRLING, THE OCHIL HILLS, DOLLAR AND CLACKMANNAN

55 MILES – 2 HOURS
START AND FINISH IN STIRLING

The royal burgh of Stirling sits at the historical and geographical heart of Scotland, within easy reach of both Highlands and Lowlands. This varied tour combines the scenic delights of the Ochil Hills and the Forth Valley, with the historic sites of Sheriff Muir, Castle Campbell and Clackmannan. It also visits the Dunmore Pineapple, one of the most unusual buildings in Scotland. Parts of this tour follow narrow, twisting roads across hills that may be closed by snow in winter.

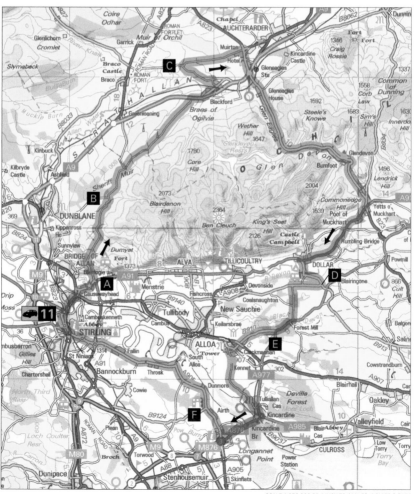

SCALE 1:250 000 OR 1 INCH TO 4 MILES *1 CM TO 2.5 KM*

From the roundabout beside the old bridge in Stirling city centre take the A9 across the river towards Bridge of Allan. At the roundabout go straight across, following signs for the Wallace Monument to the car park at the top of the hill. Turn right out of the monument car park. The road heads downhill and bends sharply right just before joining the A91; turn left here **A** on a very narrow road signposted Logie Kirk. The road twists up a steep hill. Turn right at the T-junction at the top. From a parking area a short distance beyond the junction, a walk of about a mile and a half takes you up a ridge to the summit of Dumyat (1,373 feet, 418m), the most westerly peak in the Ochil Hills. **The road continues across the moor to the lonely Sheriffmuir Inn B where the road bends to the right and goes straight uphill.** At the top of this slope is the ruined farmhouse of Lairhill and downhill to the left is the site of the famous Battle of Sheriff Muir, which took place during the ill-fated Jacobite Rising of 1715. The battle itself, between the pro-Hanoverian forces of the Duke of Argyll and the Jacobite army of the Earl of Mar, was inconclusive, but it marked the end of the uprising. The second half of the road has numerous parking places which make good picnic spots. In late summer, the moor is a vast purple carpet of heather, with the spectacular backdrop of the Southern Highlands spread out to the north.

Where the Sheriff Muir road meets the A9 turn right, then exit left on the B8081 to Blackford. This village has long been famous for the quality of its water which bubbles out of springs at the northern edge of the Ochil Hills; and it was here that Scotland's first public brewery went into operation. Today the mineral water from Blackford's springs is bottled at

The Old Bridge and Wallace Monument, Stirling

source and sold all over the world. **Cross the level crossing at the far end of the village and turn immediately and sharply to the left. Turn left at a little crossroads, then right at a T-junction C.** After a mile or two you begin to catch glimpses of a golfcourse through the curtain of trees on the righthand side of the road – one of two courses associated with the world-famous Gleneagles Hotel whose entrance is slightly further along. **At the 'stop' sign beyond the Gleneagles Hotel turn right onto the A823 towards Glen Eagles and Glen Devon.**

The road climbs into the narrow, steep-sided defile of Glen Eagles. The name has nothing to do with birds of prey, but derives from the Gaelic word *eaglais*, meaning 'church', and referring to the chapel of St Mungo which

once sat at the foot of the glen. As you approach the pass at 882 feet above sea level, there is a fine view back down the glen, with Gleneagles Hotel prominent in the distance. This route is the principal pass through the Ochil Hills which form a barrier stretching from Stirling to the Firth of Tay near Perth. It was once an important drove road connecting the cattle market at Crieff with south Fife.

On the far side of the pass you enter Glen Devon, a scenic valley that winds gently down to the blue expense of Castlehill Reservoir, a popular picnic spot. **At the foot of Glen Devon, 12 miles from the Gleneagles Hotel, turn right on the A91 towards Dollar and Stirling.** The village at the mouth of the glen is called Yetts o' Muckhart, meaning 'swineherds' gates', a reminder that there was once a drover's

Glen Devon

tollhouse here. **In Dollar, turn right at the little clocktower by the bridge over the stream (the road to be taken is signposted for Castle Campbell). As the road begins to climb the hill, fork left in front of The Village Shop (there's another sign for Castle Campbell here, but it is very inconspicuous).**

Return to the main road in Dollar and turn right, then

• PLACES OF INTEREST •

Stirling

Few towns have played as important a part in Scottish history as Stirling. Its fine castle, commanding the route north from Edinburgh and the south towards the Highlands and the northeast, was a royal palace and the seat of Scottish government from the fifteenth to the seventeenth centuries, and before that it was the site of many pivotal battles, including the Battle of Stirling Bridge in 1297 and Bannockburn in 1314, both major victories for the Scots. The bridge that Wallace defended in 1297 is no more, but the Auld Brig which was built around 1500 still survives. One of the four arches was demolished in 1745 to hold off Bonnie Prince Charlie's troops, but it was later rebuilt.

The old town spreads along the ridge below the castle, and contains a number of fine old buildings. Argyll Lodging, on Castle Wynd, is one of the country's finest seventeenth-century town houses, and now serves as a youth hostel. Across the way is Mar's Wark, a Renaissance mansion built in 1570 for the Earl of Mar, its ornate façade decorated with heraldic panels. The infant James VI was crowned in the nearby Church of the Holy Rude in 1567, while John Knox preached the sermon.

Stirling Castle. The royal fortress of Stirling occupies a magnificent position on a black basalt crag, with grand views across the historical and geographical heart of Scotland. The principal buildings, most of

which date from the sixteenth to the eighteenth centuries, cluster around two courtyards. The Palace, built for James V in the 1540s, is decorated on the outside with a series of grotesque statues and gargoyles, including a representation of the devil. The interior of the Chapel Royal, where the infant Mary Queen of Scots was crowned in 1543, has a high wooden ceiling covered with seventeenth-century painting. The neighbouring Great Hall, which dates from around 1500, is one of the most impressive halls in Scotland, especially now that it has been restored to its former splendour. It is 126 feet long, 37 feet wide, and 54 feet high, and covered by a magnificent hammer-beam roof. On the plain to the south of the castle you can see the King's Knot, the earthworks of a splendid formal garden laid out for Charles I in 1628.

Open April–September, daily 9.30–6; October–March, daily 9.30–5 (last ticket sold 45 minutes before closing). Telephone: (01786) 450000.

Wallace Monument

Perched on top of Abbey Craig, the Wallace Monument towers 220 feet above the summit of the hill, affording spectacular views over Stirling and the valley of the Forth. Built between 1859 and 1869, it houses an exhibition that tells the story of William Wallace, the national hero who fought for Scotland's freedom 700 years ago. The objects on display include Wallace's original two-handed

sword. Open April–October, daily 10–5 (6 in July and August). Telephone: (01786) 475019.

Castle Campbell

This castle, which enjoys one of southeast Scotland's most romantic settings, was built in the fifteenth century as the lowland seat of Colin Campbell, the first Earl of Argyll. Originally known as Castle Gloom, and set between the Burn of Sorrow and the Burn of Despair, it is not surprising that he changed its name. There is a beautiful walk of about a mile up Dollar Glen from the village to the castle, which has a tearoom nearby. Open April–September, Monday–Saturday 9.30–6.30, Sundays 2–6.30; October–March, Monday–Saturday 9.30–4.30, Sundays 2–4.30 (closed Thursday afternoons and Fridays). Telephone: (01259) 742408.

Clackmannan

The mysterious 'Stone of Mannan' (or Clach Mannan in Gaelic) rests on a pillar in the village square and gives its name to the former county town of Scotland's smallest county. The stone was associated with the worship of a prehistoric sea god called Mannan. Next to the stone is the seventeenth-century Mercat Cross and the sixteenth-century Tolbooth tower. A short walk west from the Tolbooth is Clackmannan Tower, the former seat of an illegitimate grandson of Robert the Bruce, whose descendants continued to live here until 1773.

take the third turning on the left (Devon Road), signposted B913 Kincardine Bridge. As the road climbs across a wooded hillside, turn right **D** onto the B9140 towards Coalsnaughton. Ahead you can see the great southern scarp of the Ochils, defined by a major geological fault separating resistant volcanic rocks to the north from softer sedimentary rocks to the south. Along its foot lies a string of towns – Tillicoultry, Alva and Menstrie – that took advantage of the fast streams tumbling from the hills to power their woollen mills in the nineteenth century. **At a row of red-tiled cottages turn left on a minor road signposted Aberdona. Turn right at the T-junction at the foot of the hill onto the A977.** Less than a mile later, you pass signs for a lefthand bend and a T-junction; look out for an inconspicuous sign on the left side of the road pointing to the B910. **Turn right here E, beside a small car park with a tourist information board.** The town of Clackmannan is visible ahead, with the prominent Clackmannan Tower capping the ridge above it. **At the T-junction in Clackmannan turn right**

The Dunmore Pineapple

Dollar Glen

towards Alloa, then turn left at the Tower Inn to reach a square with a clocktower and old market cross.

Go straight across the square and down the hill. The route descends onto the level floodplain of the River Forth, with the twin chimneys of Kincardine Power Station rising ahead. **The road goes past the power station, then turns left at the end of a row of old cottages. Turn right then right again into Kincardine town centre.** Formerly an important port and shipbuilding centre, the town is now best known for its swing bridge, which was the lowest bridging point on the Forth until the Forth Road Bridge was opened in 1964. **Turn right at the T-junction below the clocktower and cross Kincardine Bridge on the A876. At the roundabout turn right on the A905.** During medieval times Airth was the port for Stirling, and the site of the royal shipyard. Fifteenth-century

Airth Castle, prominent on a wooded hill to the left of the road, is now a hotel. **Go through Airth and turn left on the B9124 towards Cowie, then immediately right to visit the Dunmore Pineapple F.**

The Pineapple is probably the most peculiar piece of architecture in Scotland. It was built in 1761 as a garden retreat by an unknown architect. It overlooks an orchard garden where pineapples are thought to have been grown in glasshouses along the south wall during the eighteenth century. The building is not open to the public, but is leased as a holiday home. **Return to the A905 and turn left.** This final stretch of road between South Alloa and Fallin offers grand views across the Forth to the Ochils and the Highland peaks of Ben Vorlich and Stuc a' Chroin, and ahead to the distinctive silhouette of Stirling Castle perched on its crag. **Continue on the A905 to return to the centre of Stirling.** ■

BANNOCKBURN, THE ANTONINE WALL AND THE CAMPSIE FELLS

57 MILES – 3 HOURS
START AND FINISH IN STIRLING

The expansion of the Roman empire in Britain stopped with the building of the Antonine Wall across the 'waist' of Scotland. Here too, Robert the Bruce stopped the English at the Battle of Bannockburn and sent them home 'to think again'. This tour visits the site of the battlefield before heading south to follow the line of the Roman wall, which is paralleled for much of its length by the Forth and Clyde Canal. The return leg climbs high over the Campsie Fells to the pretty village of Fintry and ends with a spectacular view over Stirling and the Forth valley. This route is not recommended in winter when snow may block the roads over the Campsie Fells.

From the roundabout in Stirling city centre take the A9 south towards St Ninians and Bannockburn. Pass straight across two more roundabouts, ending on the A872 to Denny. One and a half miles after starting you pass a service station on the right and immediately beyond is the inconspicuous entrance to the Bannockburn Heritage Centre **A**.

Continue out of town, cross the motorway (M9, junction 9), and take the second minor road on the left towards Plean. After a short distance the road passes a school house on the left then runs straight for nearly a mile, following the exact line of an old Roman road. This road once connected the Roman fort on the Antonine Wall at Falkirk with the fort at Braco (see Tour 14). **At the crossroads B turn left to visit Plean Country Park.** The grounds of Plean House, once the home of William Simpson, a wealthy nineteenth-century

merchant, are now a public park with wooded walks, a walled garden and picnic tables. The old house is a ruin (though it was lived in as recently as 1970) but the grounds are attractive with varied woodland, wildflower meadows, a pond and a stream.

Return to the Roman road and continue to the A9 at the village of Torwood and turn right. Go straight across a roundabout towards Falkirk. Turn left at the T-junction, then right at another roundabout (second exit) beside the Rosebank Inn C, and immediately right onto the B816 (Glenfour Road) which runs alongside the Forth and Clyde Canal. This is the eastern end of the canal which once linked the Firth of Forth with the Firth of Clyde on the west coast. Uphill to the left is the Falkirk end of the Union Canal (see Tour 2) which leads to Edinburgh, and which was originally linked to the Forth and Clyde. **Pass the flight of canal**

locks and take the second street on the right (Tamfourhill Road); 300 yards along on the left is the entrance to Watling Lodge. Here you can see the best surviving stretch of the ditch that ran along the north side of the Antonine Wall. Even after the passage of nearly 2,000 years, the ditch is still almost 40 feet wide and 15 feet deep. Set back about 20 feet away from the southern lip, a low ridge shows the line where the original turf rampart stood.

Continue along this road (B816) for 3 miles to Bonnybridge. As you descend through the town, look out for the Antonine Primary School on your left. Opposite the school an inconspicuous signpost for Rough Castle points down a minor road on the right; this deteriorates to an unsurfaced farm track after one mile, but leads to a parking area – where the track bends right, go left

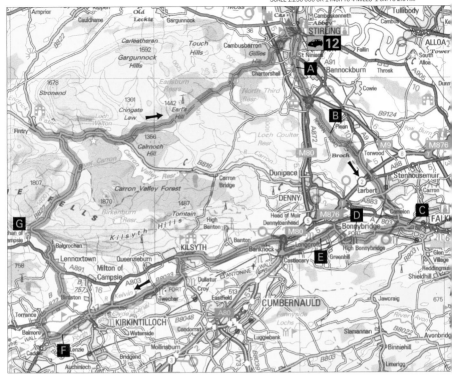

through a gate with a cattle grid and continue to some trees D. Rough Castle, which lies a few hundred yards beyond the parking area, is the best preserved of the Roman forts that

guarded the Antonine Wall, and originally provided barracks accommodation for about 500 soldiers. Even so, there is little to see other than a few ditches and earthworks, but information

boards help the imagination to fill in the gaps. Almost a mile of wall and ditch survives here, the wall still nearly 5 feet high in places. **Return to the main road, turn right, and take the first road**

• PLACES OF INTEREST •

Stirling
For information see Tour 11.

Bannockburn
The most decisive battle in the wars between England and Scotland was fought at this place on the 23 and 24 June 1314. Stirling Castle, held by an English garrison, was under siege, and the English commander had agreed to surrender to the Scots if he had not been relieved by Midsummer Day. Accordingly, Edward II marched north towards Stirling with a force of over 18,000 men. The Scottish army, under their commanders Robert the Bruce, his brother Edward, Thomas Randolph (Earl of Moray), 'Good Sir James' Douglas, and Robert Keith, waited

for them on a ridge above the Bannock Burn, about two miles south of the castle. Although the Scots were outnumbered, Edward II's tactics were poor, and with the advantage of the high ground Bruce's forces drove the English

back into the bogs around the burn. Edward fled and his army disintegrated. Bannockburn was a great victory for the Scots, confirming the position of Bruce as king, and leading to the recognition of Scotland as an independent nation, although the surly English did not conclude a peace treaty until 1328. The site is now in the care of the National Trust for Scotland, and in the adjacent visitor centre an audio-visual presentation recreates the progress of the battle. Battle site open at all times. Visitor centre open April–October, daily 10–5.30; November–March, daily 11–3 (closed 23 December–28 February). Telephone: (01786) 812664.

on the left immediately before the canal bridge (still the B816). After half a mile both road and canal cross a stream, and here on the left is a gate leading to the Seabegs Wood stretch of the Antonine Wall . Here you can see another length of ditch and rampart and, set back about 20 yards from the ditch to the south, a raised but grass-covered road. This is part of the 'Military Way', the cobbled Roman road that ran the length of the wall, allowing the legionnaires to march from fort to fort.

Continue to the intersection at Castlecary, and follow signs for Stirling A80 north across the bridge, then exit left, and turn right on the A803 towards Kilsyth. As you reach the edge of Kilsyth, you will see a minor road on the right prominently signposted for Colzium House/Lennox Estate. It was at Kilsyth, in 1645, that the royalist Highlanders of James Graham, Marquis of Montrose, won a famous victory over the Covenanters, only to be themselves defeated a month later at Philiphaugh, near Selkirk. In

Forth and Clyde Canal

Kilsyth town centre turn left on the B802 towards Cumbernauld and Airdrie. Just before the road crosses the Forth and Clyde Canal, turn right onto the B8023 towards Kirkintilloch. From Twechar, about a mile and a half after this junction, there is a circular walk of 6 miles that heads east along the canal towpath to Craigmarloch (the second bridge), and returns through Croy along the line of the Antonine Wall. **The car route**

follows the canal bank to the A803, where it turns left along the edge of Kirkintilloch, heading for Bishopbriggs. It crosses over the canal at Glasgow Bridge . Both the road and the Antonine Wall cross the line of the canal at this point, beside a pleasant country pub.

Turn right at the roundabout beyond the bridge onto the A807, and then after three quarters of a mile turn right again at the village of Torrance, onto the B822 heading for Lennoxtown. The town was established in the late eighteenth century as a coalmining and textile centre. The southern slopes of the Campsie Fells rise steeply behind the town. Here you go left along the A891 for just over a half mile before turning right on the B822 towards Fintry. This road passes the village green before climbing steeply up to a car park and viewpoint above Campsie Glen . The view extends southward over the whole of the Central Lowlands. The Campsie Fells, a high plateau

• PLACES OF INTEREST •

Antonine Wall
The Roman invasion of Scotland in AD 83–84 was stopped at the southern edge of the Highlands by the difficult terrain and the savage attacks of the native Picts. The Romans returned the following century, and built the Antonine Wall to defend the remote northwestern frontier of their vast empire. The wall, built around 142 at the command of the Roman emperor Antoninus Pius, consisted of a wide ditch backed by a turf rampart and timber parapet, with forts every two miles and a military road running along the south side. It runs from Old Kilpatrick (on the Clyde, just west of Glasgow) to Carriden, east of Bo'ness, on the Firth of Forth, a distance of 37 miles. It was abandoned by the end

of the second century AD, but despite 2,000 years of erosion there are still long stretches of visible ditch and rampart.

Colzium House
The nineteenth-century country home of the Edmonstones of Duntreath now houses a museum of local history. The landscaped grounds contain a walled garden, a couple of small lochs, and the ruins of Colzium Castle, razed by Cromwell's troops in the seventeenth century. Grounds open daily, dawn to dusk. Telephone: (01236) 823281.

Forth and Clyde Canal
The first of Scotland's canals to be cut, the Forth and Clyde took 22 years of work before it was finally

opened in 1790. It stretches 39 miles from Bowling on the Clyde to Grangemouth on the Forth, rises to 150 feet above sea level, and had 40 locks (some of which have since been filled in). It was once the busiest canal in the country, but decreasing use in the twentieth century led to it being abandoned in 1962. Several stretches, notably in Glasgow and Grangemouth, have been filled in, but much of it is still navigable and there are plans to re-open the entire length of the canal in the near future. The towpath is maintained, and provides pleasant country walks. For further information contact British Waterways, telephone: (0141) 332 6936.

Culcreuch Castle grounds

composed of layers of volcanic rock, form a barrier to communication stretching from the Clyde to Stirling; the highest point is Earl's Seat (1,897 feet, 578m) at the western end. This road, known as the 'Crow Road', crosses the high, grassy summit of the Campsies at a height of over 1,000 feet (300m) with grand views of the Trossachs and the Highlands to the north to be seen from the top.

Continue across the hills to reach Fintry. Set on the south bank of the Endrick Water, the pretty, flower-bedecked village of Fintry was founded in the late eighteenth century to provide accommodation for workers at a cotton mill built by the owner of nearby Culcreuch Castle. 'Old' Fintry, centred on the little parish kirk about a mile upstream, has been a hill farming hamlet since the thirteenth century. Sixteenth-century Culcreuch Castle, the ancestral seat of the Galbraiths, is now a hotel, but the 1,600 acre (648 hectare) grounds are open to the public. **Return the way you came for a mile, then turn left on the B818 towards Denny. The road climbs up the valley of the Endrick Water.** The road crosses a bridge over the Endrick Water a few hundred yards upstream from the Loup of Fintry, an attractive

waterfall where the river drops 95 feet over a series of rocky ledges into a gorge. **Beyond the bridge, the road passes beneath the parapet of the Carron Valley Reservoir on the right. At the far end of the dam the route bears left on a minor road (not signposted, but there is a sign prohibiting vehicles over 7.5 tons).** This is a single track road with passing places; beware of sheep and lambs. **A few hundred yards after turning up this road, a rough forestry road on the right leads to a picnic area.** This grassy clearing above the loch enjoys a fine view across the Carron Valley Reservoir to the conical peak of Meikle Bin. At the far end are the earthworks of an

ancient motte, a castle rampart that was once capped with a timber palisade. This one, which belonged to Sir John de Graham (who died while fighting for Wallace's cause at the Battle of Falkirk in 1298) is unusual in being square – most mottes of this age are circular.

Return to the minor road and continue across the hills. The little road winds its way across the hills, passing some pleasant summer picnic spots, then descends towards Stirling. On a fine summer evening you will be rewarded with a spectacular panorama over the city, the Ochil Hills and the Forth valley. **Follow signs on minor roads back towards Stirling city centre.** ■

Statue of Robert the Bruce, Stirling Castle

DUNFERMLINE, LOCH LEVEN, FALKLAND AND THE SOUTH FIFE COAST

56 MILES – 2½ HOURS
START AND FINISH IN DUNFERMLINE

The royal retreats of Dunfermline and Falkland form the two poles of this tour around south Fife and Kinross. The route takes in Loch Leven, in whose island castle Mary Queen of Scots was kept prisoner for almost a year, and the tramping country of the Lomond Hills, before returning through the seaside towns of the south Fife coast. At Aberdour you have the opportunity of taking a boat trip to Inchcolm, the 'Iona of the East'.

From the roundabout in Dunfermline at the junction of the A907 and A823, take the minor road north signposted Townhill and Kingseat. Where this road bends sharply right **A** go straight on towards Townhill, passing the Town Loch on the left. The road continues to a T-junction with the B915, where you turn right. Just over 1 mile later you join the B914 to Kelty, but turn immediately left **B** on a minor road to Cleish. The road climbs over the Cleish Hills through dense forestry plantations. Loch Glow Country Park has a parking and picnic area, and is the starting point for walks in the hills. As the road descends to the north, there is a magnificent view over Loch Leven to the Lomond Hills.

As the road descends the far side of the hills you meet two T-junctions in quick succession – go right then left. About a mile to the left of the first junction lies Cleish Castle, where Mary Queen of Scots was

---

• PLACES OF INTEREST •

Dunfermline
The town's name means 'the fort by the crooked stream' and, although the original fort has long since crumbled to dust, the crooked stream of the Pittencrieff Burn still flows beneath the ruins of the abbey and palace founded by Malcolm Canmore and his queen, the saintly Margaret, in the eleventh century. Dunfermline was for many centuries a favourite royal residence and, following Queen Margaret's canonisation in 1250, a place of pilgrimage. The abbey church was the burial place of eight Scottish kings including Robert the Bruce, four queens, five princes and two princesses. A nineteenth-century neo-Gothic church is attached to the graceful twelfth-century Romanesque nave of the abbey church founded by David I. Across the road, the

impressive remains of the abbey buildings, and the royal palace where Charles I was born, overlook the attractive gardens of Pittencrieff Park gifted to the town by its most famous son, Andrew Carnegie.

Born in Dunfermline in 1835, the son of a poor weaver, Carnegie emigrated to the USA in 1848 and began a career which made him a leading industrialist and one of the richest men in the world. He spent his great fortune on philanthropic projects, including educational trusts and free public libraries – his total benefactions have been estimated at $350 million. To his home town he gave, as well as Pittencrieff Park (from which he had been barred as a boy), its own Carnegie Library, a public baths, and several trusts which continue to benefit the public to this day.

Dunfermline Abbey. Open April–September, Monday–Saturday 9.30–6.30, Sundays 2–6.30; October–March, Monday–Saturday 9.30–4.30, Sundays 2–4.30; closed Thursday afternoons and Fridays in winter. Telephone: (01383) 739026.
Abbot's House. This historic building, which was once the residence of the abbot of Dunfermline, has been restored as a colourful and lively museum of local history. Open daily 10–5. Telephone: (01383) 733266.
Andrew Carnegie Birthplace Museum. The weaver's cottage where the great philanthropist was born now houses a museum devoted to his life and works. Open April–October, Monday–Saturday 11–5, Sundays 2–5; November–March, daily 2–4. Telephone: (01383) 724302.

taken immediately after her escape from Loch Leven Castle. **Three hundred yards later the road bends sharply left at a farm, but go straight on towards Kinross. Just after the road passes under the motorway, turn left at a T-junction onto the B996 into Kinross.** This is a quiet little town, with a small museum and a few historic buildings. The main attraction is Loch Leven Castle. **When you can see a church tower on the left, turn right down a small road signposted Loch Leven Castle. Where the road forks, bear left (framed by signs saying 'weight limit 2 tons') and continue past a lochside park to the car park next to the jetty.** Just to the north of the car park is Kinross House, one of Scotland's finest country mansions, built by William Bruce (who designed the early part of Hopetoun House) in the late eighteenth century. The

house is not open to the public, but the magnificent landscaped gardens can be visited in summer. Loch Leven is the biggest loch in central Scotland, covering an area of around 4,000 acres (1,620 hectares). It is also one of Scotland's most famous trout-fishing lochs, and an important feeding ground and sanctuary for swans, ducks and geese. Each autumn flocks of geese numbering about 15,000 birds fly in to winter on the loch, a truly spectacular sight.

Return to the High Street and turn left, heading down the west side of the loch on the B996. When an obelisk monument comes into view on the right C turn left on the B9097 towards Glenrothes. A few miles along this road is the RSPB's Vane Farm nature reserve, which provides nature trails and hides for observing the bird life on the loch. There is also an exhibition

Dunfermline Abbey

describing the local wildlife and geology. Birds are not the only thing you might see in the skies above Loch Leven. On the east shore is Portmoak airfield, the headquarters of the Scottish Gliding Union. The prevailing westerly winds are forced upwards by the huge slope of

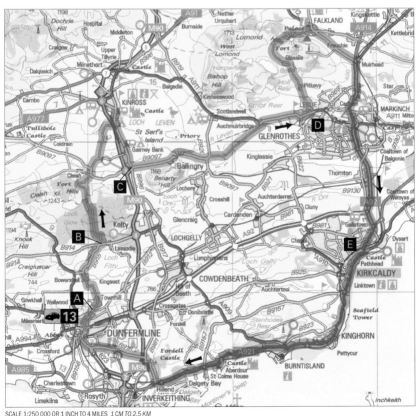

SCALE 1:250 000 OR 1 INCH TO 4 MILES *1 CM TO 2.5 KM*

63

Ravenscraig Park, Kircaldy

Bishop Hill, and the gliders ride this wave of lifting air until they can catch a thermal (a column of warm, rising air) which will take them even higher.

At a T-junction, go left towards Glenrothes. Cross Auchmuir Bridge and turn right towards the town of Leslie. On the village green in Leslie lies the 'Bull Stone', a reminder of the cruel sport of bull-baiting which was carried on here until it was banned in 1835. The bull was chained to the stone, while dogs tried to bite the poor beast on the nose. The stone is deeply grooved with chain and rope marks. **Leslie's main street bends sharp right then left. Soon after passing a church spire on the left, turn left down a minor road D signposted to Falkland and Lomond Hills.** This scenic little road climbs up to a parking place from which you can walk to the summits of both East and West Lomond; the latter is the higher, at 1,713 feet (522m). The road then drops steeply into the attractive village of Falkland.

At the T-junction in Falkland turn right towards Kirkcaldy on the A912. This leads to a roundabout, where you take the A92 dual carriageway to Kirkcaldy. Six and a half miles later you reach another roundabout on the edge of Kirkcaldy. Take the first exit, signposted Kirkcaldy East. Go straight across the next roundabout, and right at a third one E, towards the Town Centre. If you turn left here, you will see a car park on the right signposted Ravenscraig Castle. From here you can visit the ruin of the fifteenth-century fortress. Situated on top of a promontory above the sea, the two huge towers facing the land have walls 14 feet thick, connected by a curtain wall. **Continue through Kirkcaldy.** Known as 'the Lang Toun', Kirkcaldy's main street is over 3 miles long. It is the biggest town in Fife, and during the nineteenth century it was famous for its linoleum factories. The route passes the harbour, and continues along the promenade beside a long, sandy beach. **At the roundabout at the far end of the prom, turn left on the A921 coast road towards Kinghorn and Burntisland.**

The pleasant little town of Kinghorn once made its living from spinning and shipbuilding. By the road to the west of town stands a memorial to Alexander III who died here in 1286 when his horse stumbled over the cliffs on a dark, stormy night. Burntisland was once a busy industrial port, but is now being developed as a resort. Rossend Castle, overlooking the harbour, was once held by Rob Roy MacGregor in the name of the Old Pretender, but it is more famous for the visit of Mary Queen of Scots in 1563. On this occasion a French poet, Pierre Chastelard was found hiding in the queen's bed-chamber. It was not his first offence – he had done the same thing at Holyrood Palace. The

Falkland Palace

The Silver Sands, Aberdour

queen pardoned him the first time, but on the second he was found guilty of *lèse-majesté* and executed. **At the roundabout in Burntisland turn left towards Aberdour.**

From Aberdour continue on the A921 towards the Forth Road Bridge. Go straight across the roundabout at Dalgety Bay, then turn right at the next

roundabout on the B916 through Hillend. At a T-junction turn right, then almost immediately turn left back towards Dunfermline on the B916. ■

• PLACES OF INTEREST •

Loch Leven Castle
This well-preserved fourteenth-century tower is famous as having been the place where Mary Queen of Scots was imprisoned after her surrender at Carberry Hill in 1567. She remained incarcerated here for almost a year, until she escaped with the help of the young boatman, Willie Douglas. In Mary's time the loch was much larger and the castle island much smaller; the loch was partly drained in the seventeenth century by Sir William Bruce, in order to provide land for a landscape garden in front of Kinross House.

Open April–September, Monday–Saturday 9.30–6.30, Sundays 2–6.30. Telephone: (0131) 668 8600.

Vane Farm RSPB Visitor Centre
Open daily 10–5 (4 in January–March). Telephone: (01577) 862355.

Falkland
This pretty village, in the shadow of East Lomond Hill, was a favourite hunting retreat of Stuart monarchs from James I to James VI, but fell into neglect after the Union of the Crowns when James VI went south to London. The medieval village's

raison d'être was the magnificent Royal Palace built between 1502–41. It is a fine example of early Renaissance architecture and incorporates the oldest 'Real Tennis' court in the world, which is still in use today. The village retains its medieval layout, and many of the houses date from the seventeenth and eighteenth centuries. Visitors are catered for by several tearooms and there are a couple of antique shops.

Royal Palace. Open April–late October, Monday–Saturday 11–5.30, Sundays 1.30–5.30. Telephone: (01337) 857397.

Aberdour
On summer weekends, day trippers from Edinburgh flock to the silver sands of Aberdour to enjoy the beach and the bracing sea air, a tradition which began back in Victorian times when the town began to develop as a resort. Before the nineteenth century, however, Aberdour was a working town with a busy harbour, earning its keep from salt-panning, quarrying and weaving. It has long been the seat of the Earls of Morton who still live here.

Aberdour Castle dates from the fourteenth century when these

lands were first granted to the Earl of Morton by Robert the Bruce. It was added to in the sixteenth and seventeenth centuries and has a fine walled garden with an unusual sixteenth-century doocot shaped like a beehive. Open April–September, Monday–Saturday 9.30–6.30, Sundays 2–6.30; October–March, Monday–Saturday 9.30–4.30, Sundays 2–4.30; closed Thursday afternoons and Fridays in winter. Telephone: (01383) 860519.

Inchcolm
Known as the 'Iona of the East', this little island in the Firth of Forth has one of Scotland's best-preserved medieval abbeys. It was founded by Alexander I in 1123 in gratitude for having been looked after by one of the island's hermits when he was shipwrecked there. The island is mentioned in Shakespeare's *Macbeth* as 'St Colme's Inch', where the Norwegian king Sweno was buried. It can be reached by boat from Aberdour, only a mile and a half to the north, or from South Queensferry (see Tour 2). Closed November–March. Daily sailings June–September. Check times by phone. Telephone: (01383) 860335.

DUNBLANE, COMRIE, LOCH EARN AND CALLANDER

70 MILES – 3 HOURS
START AND FINISH IN STIRLING

The town of Comrie sits astride the geological fault that separates the Highlands from the Lowlands, and has been regularly rattled by earth tremors since time immemorial. This tour also straddles the Highland boundary, heading north to Comrie through the little cathedral city of Dunblane and the Roman fort at Braco, before making a brief incursion beyond the Highland line to sample the delights of Loch Earn. It then returns to Stirling along the well-trodden tourist route through Strathyre, Callander and Doune.

Drive northward out of Stirling on the A9 towards Bridge of Allan, crossing the River Forth beside the Old Bridge A. Turn left at the roundabout below the Wallace Monument and **continue through Bridge of Allan.** There was little more than a hamlet beside the bridge over the Allan Water until the nineteenth century when a Victorian spa resort developed around the mineral springs issuing from an old copper mine. There is a pleasant walk, called the 'Daurinn Road', along the banks of the Allan Water to Dunkeld. It follows the route of an old Roman road and passes a cave which was once a favourite retreat of the novelist Robert Louis Stevenson.

At the motorway intersection beyond Bridge of Allan (M9, junction 11), the route turns right along a dual carriageway (B8033) into Dunblane. Pass through a set of traffic lights, cross the railway bridge, then turn left (signposted Town Centre). Go along the narrow High Street and across a mini-roundabout to Cathedral Square. There is a car park on the far side of the cathedral.

Go back to the mini-roundabout and turn left, then left again at a larger roundabout on the old road to Perth. After 1 mile go left on the B8033 to Kinbuck. The route now passes through the lush farmland of Strathallan, with the heathery slopes of the Sheriff Muir (see Tour 11) rising to the

Deil's Caldron

southeast. **Continue to Braco. Turn left at the T-junction and cross the bridge to find a lay-by on the left.** In the field behind the hedges opposite the parking area lies a complex of ditches and earthworks that marks the site of one of the country's largest and best-preserved Roman forts. Although the fort was probably established during Agricola's invasion of 83–84 AD, most of the remains date from the second century, the period during which the Antonine Wall was built. The buildings would have been made of timber; the stone foundations here are from a medieval church. Finds from excavations, on display in

Glasgow University's Hunterian Museum, include a tombstone whose inscription indicates that the fort's garrison included some soldiers from Spain. Beside the road bridge over the stream in Braco are the overgrown remains of a much older bridge, which may have been Roman in origin.

Half a mile beyond Braco turn left on the B827 towards Comrie. The route heads up the broad and deserted valley of the River Knaik. A few miles before Comrie it passes the entrance to the Auchingarrich Wildlife Centre, then snakes through some more hills to emerge on the flat plain of the River Earn, with the obelisk of Lord Melville's Monument

prominent on the wooded hilltop above the town. **At the T-junction in Comrie turn left on the A85 to Crianlarich. The road bends right then sharp left. To visit the Deil's Caldron turn right at the second bend on a single track road (Burrell Street) that leads up Glen Lednock to a car park B near the waterfall.** From the car park you can walk back to a footpath and long wooden staircase that leads down to a viewing platform overlooking the Deil's Cauldron, a waterfall hidden in the deep, wooded gorge of the River Lednock. Another path leads steeply up from the road to the Melville Monument, a

67

tall granite obelisk raised in memory of Henry Dundas, first Viscount Melville (1742–1811), one of the most powerful politicians of his time, who retired to a small cottage near Comrie. The magnificent views from the monument are well worth the effort of reaching it. Both the waterfall and the monument can be included in a 4-mile circular walk from a car park situated at the foot of the glen, just outside Comrie.

Leave Comrie along the A85 towards Loch Earn. The route has now crossed the Highland line and heads west into the mountains. About a mile short of St Fillans, to the left of the road, is the rocky, wooded hill of Dundurn, capped by the remains of a Pictish fort. To its west, beside the golfcourse, the ruins of a fifteenth-century chapel mark the supposed site of the cell once occupied by St Fillan, the eighth-century Irish missionary who brought Christianity to this glen. The saint's name was given to the pretty nineteenth-century estate

Loch Earn

village of St Fillans, which enjoys an idyllic setting at the east end of Loch Earn. **Just as you pass the sign announcing the village of St Fillans, turn left on a minor road signposted South Loch Earn (single track road with passing places).** This scenic road winds pleasantly along the wooded southern shore of Loch Earn, passing several appealing picnic spots. Towards the western end of the loch it crosses the lower slopes of Ben Vorlich (3,231 feet, 985m), one of the shapeliest peaks in the southern Highlands. Ardvorlich House is associated with a grisly tale in which a band of MacGregors,

having fallen foul of the King's forester, murdered him. They then delivered the unfortunate fellow's severed head to his sister, who was the lady of Ardvorlich House. Nearby is a tombstone that commemorates seven MacDonalds of Glencoe who died in an attack on the house in 1620.

Turn left at the junction with the main A84 road just south of Lochearnhead. After 2 miles turn left at the Kingshouse Hotel C , then turn right, passing beneath the main road towards Balquhidder. The kirkyard at Balquhidder contains the graves of the famous outlaw Rob Roy MacGregor, his wife and two of his sons, and has become something of a place of pilgrimage for MacGregors from all over the world. The little church beside the grave dates from the seventeenth century, but sits on the foundations of an even older, thirteenth-century, building. The nearby nineteenth-century kirk contains various relics of the seventeenth-century church, including the bell, Gaelic bibles, an eighth- or ninth-century grave

---

• PLACES OF INTEREST •

Stirling
For information see Tour 11.

Dunblane
According to local tradition, St Blane founded a church here on the banks of the Allan Water around the year 600. The cathedral that now dominates the town was begun in the thirteenth century, and incorporated an older tower – the lower, red sandstone part dates from around 1100. The fine Gothic building was badly damaged during the Reformation and the nave stood roofless for 300 years, but it was fully restored in the 1890s and is still in use. Inside, at the west end, there are fifteenth-century oak misericord stalls carved with various figures including centaurs and other grotesque creatures lurking in a profusion of elaborate foliage. The pews and choir stalls of Scots oak were made in the late

nineteenth and early twentieth centuries and are decorated with an endless variety of plant and animal figures, each one unique.

The Dean's House, on the corner of Cathedral Square, dates from 1624, and now contains a museum detailing the history of the cathedral from the time of St Blane to the present day. Open June–September, Monday–Saturday 10.30–12.30 and 2.30–4.30. Telephone: (01786) 824254.

Auchingarrich Wildlife Centre
This former farm can boast a veritable menagerie of birds and beasts including Highland cattle, wild deer, goats, llamas, wallabies, over 100 species of waterfowl, ornamental and game birds, and a unique wild bird hatchery. Picnic tables and adventure playground. Open daily 10–dusk. Telephone: (01764) 679469.

Rob Roy's grave

slab (supposedly that of St Angus), and an unusual font in the shape of a boulder with a hollowed out top.

Just beyond Balquhidder kirkyard, cross a small bridge and turn left (signposted Stronvar). Cross another bridge to a fork in the road; turn right to visit the Balquhidder Visitor Centre. The route forks left and then left again towards Stroneslaney. This single track road passes through two farm gates (be sure to close them behind you) D before climbing into the forest and then descending to the river at Strathyre. Rejoin the A84 and turn right. The route heads south along the shores of Loch Lubnaig. The glen is swathed in plantations of conifers and the Forestry Commission has provided several car parks, picnic areas and forest walks, all clearly signposted. A dismantled railway track on the

Doune village

far side of the loch has been converted into a footpath and cycle track that runs all the way from Strathyre to Callander. About a mile beyond the south end of the loch is a car park with a footpath leading to the spectacular Falls of Leny.

The route now passes through the heart of tourist territory, the town of Callander being a favourite stopping place for day trippers and coach parties. The

road between here and Stirling can be very busy, especially on summer weekends. Seven miles beyond Callander is the village of Doune with its splendid castle, and a few miles beyond that the entrance to Blair Drummond Safari Park. On the final stretch along the Carse of Stirling there is a good view of Stirling Castle perched on its black basalt crag. **Follow the A84 all the way back to Stirling.** ■

• PLACES OF INTEREST •

Comrie
This small town sits astride the Highland Boundary Fault, the geological dividing line between the Highlands and Lowlands. Victorian geologists flocked to set up the first seismographs here, recording over 7,300 tremors in the 1830s, and there are still occasionally very small movements of the fault. None has been serious though and even the strongest tremors do little more than rattle the crockery. Just west of the town is the tiny Earthquake House, built in 1874 as a seismic observatory. It has been restored and contains a model of a Victorian seismometer, as well as modern recording equipment. It is not open to the public but the cramped interior can be easily seen through the window and glazed doors.

The Scottish Tartans Museum, in Drummond Street, has exhibits on the history of Highland dress, the use of natural dyes and a reconstruction of a weaver's

cottage. It also houses the Scottish Tartan Society's collection of over 1,300 official designs. Open April–October, Monday–Saturday 10–6, Sundays 11–5; November–March, check times with office. Telephone: (01764) 670779.

Callander
For information see Tour 15.

Doune
Once noted for its livestock markets and the manufacture of firearms, the picturesque village of Doune has long since surrendered to the tourist trade. Its streets now offer tempting tearooms and antique shops.

Doune Castle is the town's main attraction – a magnificent and rare example of a fourteenth-century courtyard castle with a massive keep and gate tower. The castle is remarkably well preserved and has an impressive Great Hall with a carved oak screen, a minstrels'

gallery and a huge double fireplace. Open April–September, Monday–Saturday 9.30–6.30, Sundays 2–6.30; October–March, Monday–Saturday 9.30–4.30, Sundays 2–4.30; closed Thursday afternoons and Fridays in winter. Telephone: (01786) 841742.

Doune Motor Museum. Half a mile west of Doune. The museum's exhibition of vintage cars includes the second-oldest surviving Rolls-Royce in the world. Motor racing hill-climbs are held here in April, June and September. Open April–November, 10–5 (5.30 June–August). Telephone: (01786) 841203.

Blair Drummond Safari Park
A zoo without bars – lions, tigers, zebras, antelopes and many other wild animals roam free – plus a penguin pool, performing sealions and many other attractions. Open April–September, daily 10–5.30 (last admission 4.30). Telephone: (01786) 841456.

CALLANDER, THE TROSSACHS AND THE LAKE OF MENTEITH

**41 MILES – 2 HOURS
(OR 72 MILES – 3½ HOURS INCLUDING
INVERSNAID DETOUR)
START AND FINISH IN CALLANDER**

The Trossachs is one of best known areas of Scotland, famous for its beautiful landscapes of lochs and wooded hills, and for its romantic associations with Rob Roy MacGregor and Sir Walter Scott. This tour begins in the tourist town of Callander, then heads into the heart of the Trossachs. From Loch Katrine the route climbs over the Duke's Road to Aberfoyle where a long detour leads into the remote homeland of Rob Roy. The return leg visits pretty Gartmore, then crosses Flanders Moss to the lovely Lake of Menteith with its island priory. This tour is especially recommended for late October, when the woods provide a magnificent display of autumn colours.

Head west out of Callander on the A84 towards Crianlarich. After 1 mile, in the hamlet of Kilmahog, turn left on the A821 to Aberfoyle and The Trossachs. The 250-year-old Kilmahog Woollen Mill still retains a working waterwheel, although the mill is now mainly used as a shop selling local crafts and gifts. The first part of the tour cuts along the lower slopes of Ben Ledi, above the waters of Loch Venachar, and through the hamlet of Brig o' Turk, whose curious name derives from the Gaelic *tuirc*, meaning 'wild boar'. The road then dives into the woods beside little Loch Achray. **At the far end of the loch, just beyond the Trossachs Hotel is the Ben A'an car park.** From the car park, a walk of about a mile leads to the summit of the pointed, rocky little peak called Ben A'an, where you can enjoy a magnificent view over Loch Katrine and the very heart of the Trossachs.

A few hundred yards beyond the car park, turn right. This cul-de-sac leads in 1 mile to a car park at the east end of Loch Katrine. The SS *Sir Walter Scott* departs daily from the adjacent Trossachs pier for cruises along the loch to Stronachlachar. The road that runs along the north shore of the loch is closed to traffic, but walkers and cyclists can wander as far as they wish. **Return to the A821 and turn right towards Aberfoyle.** The route now curves around the head of Loch Achray and begins to climb over the Duke's Pass. This winding hill road was originally constructed by the local landowner, the Duke of Montrose, to cope with the influx of tourists in the mid-nineteenth century. A popular excursion from Glasgow in the 1890s was to take the train to Balloch, then the steamer along Loch Lomond to Inversnaid, where a coach would take you to Stronachlachar. From there it was another cruise, this time on Loch Katrine, to the Trossachs Pier where you would take a coach over the Duke's Pass to the railway station at Aberfoyle, and so back to Glasgow. The Achray Forest Drive is a 7-mile circular route which includes some lovely

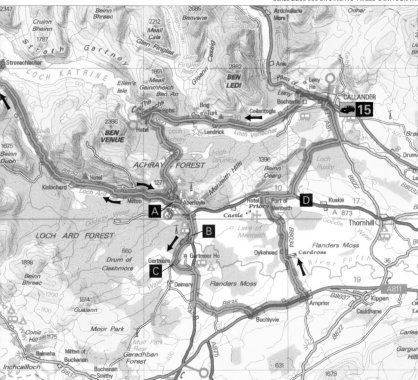

picnic spots on Loch Drunkie and Loch Achray. There are several spectacular viewpoints, with parking and picnic areas, on the main road too, which finally descends into the town of Aberfoyle.

At the foot of the hill in Aberfoyle the road bends sharp left A. Turn right here on the B829 to visit Stronachlachar and Inversnaid. This long, narrow and twisting road, single track for most of its length, cuts deep into the remote glens between lochs Lomond and Katrine, following the line of an eighteenth-century military road that once led to a fort at Inversnaid. It first squeezes along the steep shore of Loch Ard with fine views of the conical peak of Ben Lomond (3,194 feet, 974m) ahead, then passes picnic sites at lovely Loch Chon before reaching a T-junction at the head of Loch Arklet. A right turn leads to Stronachlachar on Loch Katrine, from where you can walk to Glen Gyle at the loch's head, the

birthplace of Rob Roy. A left turn leads to the shores of Loch Lomond at Inversnaid where the West Highland Way long distance footpath passes through en route

from Glasgow to Fort William. Rob Roy once farmed here, and at Craigroyston, a few miles to the south. The garrison fort above the hotel was established in an

Woods near Loch Achray

attempt to control the unruly MacGregor clan. The famous Falls of Inversnaid, immortalised in verse by William Wordsworth and Gerard Manley Hopkins, have been decreased in force by the hydroelectric dam on Loch Arklet. Both of these roads are dead-ends, and you must return to Aberfoyle the same way you came. The round trip from Aberfoyle to Inversnaid is 31 miles.

Return to Aberfoyle and turn right on the A81 towards Strathblane and Glasgow. After 1 mile turn right  on a minor road that leads to the village of Gartmore. This pretty little estate village enjoys a magnificent view of Ben Lomond to the west. The estate belonged to the family of Robert Cunninghame Graham (1852–1936), a famous politician and travel writer, who

was the first president of the Scottish Labour Party and later the first president of the Scottish National Party. There is a memorial to him beside the village green (now a football pitch). **At the far end of the village turn left  towards Glasgow. Turn right along the A81 for a mile and a half, then go left along the B835 to Buchlyvie.** Spread out to the left of the road, and now covered with forestry plantations, is the boggy peat basin of Flanders Moss. When the railway to Aberfoyle was built in the 1880s it had to be 'floated' across the bog on mats of brushwood. Excavations in the Moss have unearthed the occasional piece of whalebone, indicating that once, many thousands of years ago, it was an extension of the Firth of Forth.

Loch Katrine

Turn left onto the A811 at the T-junction in Buchlyvie. Three miles further on, at the hamlet of Arnprior, turn left again onto the B8034 towards Port of Menteith. The road follows one of the ancient routes across the Moss, following a ridge of slightly higher land, to reach the Lake of Menteith.

The road runs along the shore of the Lake of Menteith for half a mile to a parking

---

• PLACES OF INTEREST •

Callander

This thriving tourist town was developed as a fashionable spa resort in the nineteenth century when middle class Victorians would arrive by train to 'take the waters', enjoy some brisk country walks and take a cruise along Loch Katrine in a steamer. Many well known literary names, including William and Dorothy Wordsworth, Samuel Taylor Coleridge, Gerard Manley Hopkins, John Ruskin, James Hogg ('The Ettrick Shepherd'), and of course Sir Walter Scott, visited at one time or another. The area was popularised by the publication of Sir Walter Scott's *The Lady of the Lake* (which is set in the Trossachs) in 1810, and his novel *Rob Roy* in 1818, but tourism really began in earnest after the arrival of the railway in 1860s. The railway was closed down in the 1960s, but Callander remains as popular as ever, its gift shops and tearooms catering to an endless stream of visitors.

There are many pleasant walks around town. One path leads uphill behind the town to the Bracklinn Falls, where the Keltie

Water plunges into a deep gorge; another heads west out of town on the line of the old railway, passing the remains of a Roman fort at Bochastle Farm on the way to the Falls of Leny and Loch Lubnaig. Away from the busy main street, there are pleasant meadows for picnicking beside the River Teith.

Rob Roy and Trossachs Visitor Centre, housed in a former church in Ancaster Square, contains an exhibition and audio-visual presentation on the life and times of the famous outlaw Rob Roy MacGregor. Open March–May and October–December, daily 10–5; June and September, 9.30–6; July and August, 9am–10pm; January and February, weekends only, 10–5. Telephone: (01877) 330 342.

Kilmahog Woollen Mill

Open April–October, daily 9–5.30; November–March, daily 10–5. Telephone: (01877) 330268.

The Trossachs

The origin of the name 'Trossachs' has been lost in the mists of time, but it is thought to mean either 'the bristled country' or 'the crossing

hills', both of which would seem to describe this region of rocky, wooded hills and interlocking glens. The name was originally applied only to the area at the eastern end of Loch Katrine, but it is now used to describe the whole region between Loch Lomond and Callander, from Aberfoyle north to Balquhidder, which roughly coincides with 'Rob Roy' country. The famous outlaw was born near Stronachlachar at the head of Loch Katrine, and married Mary Campbell, from the remote homestead of Comer, beneath the eastern slopes of Ben Lomond. He farmed at Inversnaid, and died at a cottage at Inverlochlarig Beag, at the head of Loch Voil. His grave is in the kirkyard at Balquhidder (see Tour 14).

The Trossachs area, often promoted as 'the Highlands in miniature', is famed for its lovely scenery and good opportunities for walking, which range from easy lochside strolls to demanding hill walks on the peaks of Ben Venue, Ben Ledi and Ben Lomond. Details of marked walks and forest trails can be obtained from the tourist office in Callander.

Loch Katrine

This lovely loch in the heart of the Trossachs was the inspiration for Sir Walter Scott's famous poem *The Lady of the Lake*, and its shores were the home of the famous Scots outlaw Rob Roy MacGregor. The name of the loch is derived from 'caterans', the Highland raiders

who frequented the area in times past, or from *ceiteirein*, meaning 'furies' or 'fiends'. The loch is just under 10 miles long and less than a mile wide, and since 1859 it has provided Glasgow's water supply via a system of aqueducts and tunnels. Its level has been raised 17 feet above the original shoreline. The SS *Sir Walter Scott* has been cruising the loch since 1900, and is still powered by her original steam engines. Cruises depart daily from April to September. Telephone: (0141) 955 0128 and ask for Steamer Inquiries.

Aberfoyle

This town is the southern gateway to the Trossachs, set on the banks of the infant River Forth, and has a similar history to that of Callander. It is slightly less crowded than its companion resort, making a living from farming and forestry as well as tourism. There are pleasant walks nearby, along the shore of Loch Ard and in the hills above the Visitor Centre, and also to the summit of Doon Hill, a wooded prominence to the south also known as the Fairy Knowe. It is said that on this hill, a local minister was spirited away by the fairy folk in 1692.

David Marshall Visitor Centre. Run by the Forestry Commission, the centre provides information on wildlife and walking in the Queen Elizabeth Forest Park which covers much of the Trossachs area. Open Easter–October, daily 10–6. Telephone: (01877) 382258.

Scottish Wool Centre. An exhibition detailing the history of sheep farming and the wool trade in Scotland, with practical demonstrations of sheepdog handling, spinning, weaving and knitting. Open daily 10–6 (sheep displays Easter–October only). Telephone: (01877) 382850.

Inchmahome Priory

The priory can be reached by boat from the jetty at the car park in Port of Menteith. Open April–September, Monday–Saturday 9.30–6.30, Sundays 2–6.30. Telephone: (01877) 385294.

The view across Loch Achray

area on the left. This is the only body of water in Scotland that is known as a 'lake' rather than a loch. The reasons for this are obscure but it was probably due to a transcription error by a Victorian mapmaker, as it is known to have been called the 'loch of Menteith' in the early nineteenth century. The lake is famous for its trout fishing and for the Augustinian priory on the island of Inchmahome. The extensive ruins enjoy a beautiful setting on the wooded island. The five-year-old Mary Queen of Scots was sent here for safety following the Battle of Pinkie in 1547. The choir of the old church contains the graves of Robert Cunninghame Graham and his wife. **Continue into the village and turn right at the T-junction. After little more than 1 mile go left on the A81 D which leads back to Callander.** ■

A CIRCUIT OF STRATHEARN: GLEN ALMOND, CRIEFF, MUTHILL AND AUCHTERARDER

54 MILES – 3 HOURS
START AND FINISH IN PERTH

The broad valley of Strathearn stretches westward from Perth towards the old cattle-market town of Crieff, hemmed in by the Highlands to the north and the Ochil Hills to the south. Its many attractions include fine scenery, good walks, medieval churches and Roman remains. The route first heads northwest to the neighbouring valley of Glen Almond and the Sma' Glen, one of the historic gateways to the Highlands, then turns south to the River Earn and the temptations of the Glenturret Distillery at Crieff. The return leg takes in the former weaving town of Auchterarder.

Leave Perth on the A85 Crianlarich road. Cross the bridge over the A9 at the edge of town, and take the first road on the right after the roundabout to visit Huntingtower Castle. Return to the main road and turn right. As the route leaves Perth it passes close to two historic battlefields. About a mile to the left, near the village of Tibbermore, James Graham, Marquis of Montrose, led a motley band of 2,400 Highlanders and Irish into victory over a 6,000-strong army of Covenanters in 1644. Beyond the tall tower of Methven Castle, to the right of the road, was the scene of Robert the Bruce's defeat at the hands of the English Earl of Pembroke in 1306. **In the village of Methven look out for the post office on the left, then turn right on a road signposted Glenalmond. After 3½ miles, turn left at a T-junction.** The road runs west above the River Almond, past the entrance to Glenalmond College, one of Scotland's top public schools, founded in 1847. The line of high hills ahead marks the Highland Boundary Fault, the geological dividing line between the Highlands and the Central Lowlands. **At Buchanty the route joins the B8063 A.** Park in the bend of the road

Huntingtower Castle

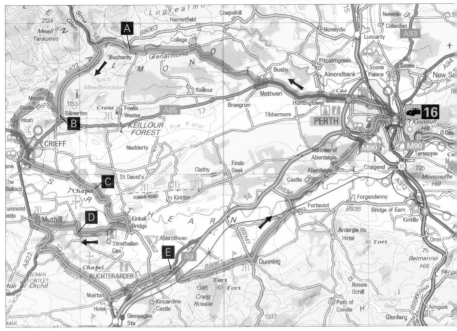

opposite the junction, and walk down to the bridge to see Buchanty Spout. A path running left from the bridge leads to a series of rocky rapids in the River Almond, where you can see salmon fighting their way upstream during the autumn run.

Go left along the B8063 to the junction with the A822. Turn right to visit the Sma' Glen. This scenic, steep-sided valley, where the River Almond carves its way out of the hills, has long been an important thoroughfare between the lowlands of Perth and the valley of Strath Tay near Aberfeldy. The prehistoric fort of Dun Mor guards the hilltop to its east, and the Romans built a fort and signal station at its mouth. General Wade drove a road through the glen, soon after Prince Charles Edward Stuart had retreated through it on his way to disaster at Culloden in 1746. During the building of Wade's road, his men moved a large stone out of the way and discovered bones beneath it. Legend maintains this was the grave of Ossian, a mythical giant. The stone can be seen about a mile and a half north of the

entrance to the glen. There are many lovely riverside picnic spots in the glen, which is particularly beautiful in late summer when the hills are purple with heather.

Return towards Crieff. As the A822 runs downhill towards the hamlet of Gilmerton, beneath the wooded slopes of the Knock of Crieff, take the small road on the right signposted Monzie and Glenturret Distillery **B**. This narrow road runs through the valley of the Shaggie Burn, and the lands of Monzie Castle, a Campbell stronghold. After a few miles you

---

• *PLACES OF INTEREST* •

Perth
For information, see Tour 18.

Huntingtower Castle
This fifteenth- to sixteenth-century castle is unusual in consisting of two separate tower houses only nine feet apart, connected by a seventeenth-century building. The gap features in the legend of the Maiden's Leap, in which Dorothea, the daughter of the first Earl of Ruthven, is said to have leapt from the roof of one tower to the next to avoid being found in her lover's bedchamber. Open April–September, Monday–Saturday 9.30–6.30, Sundays 2–6.30; October–March, Monday–Saturday 9.30–4.30, Sundays 2–4.30. Telephone: (01738) 627231.

Glenturret Distillery
Scotland's oldest Highland malt distillery, established in 1772, offers guided tours and a visitor centre, with the opportunity to sample the finished product. Shop, bar and restaurant. Open March–December, Monday–Saturday 9.30–6, Sundays 12–6; January–February, Monday–Friday 11.30–4. Telephone: (01764) 656565.

may detect a whiff of whisky in the air as you approach the warehouses of Glenturret Distillery which is open to the public for guided tours and whisky tasting. **At the junction beyond the distillery, turn left onto the A85, which takes you into Crieff.** Here the route joins the River Earn, which flows for 46 miles from its source near Lochearnhead to the Firth of Tay, just west of Newburgh. The river is famed for its trout and salmon fishing.

From the square past the tourist information office in Crieff, head downhill and turn left at the bottom on the B8062 towards Innerpeffray. After 4 miles turn right at a hen farm to visit Innerpeffray C. Here, beside the sixteenth-century Collegiate Chapel of St Mary, is Scotland's oldest free lending library, founded in the 1680s by David Drummond, the third Lord Madertie. The library contains about 3,000 books dating from before 1800, including one that was printed in 1502. There is a tearoom in the building and pleasant walks by the River Earn. At Innerpeffray the River Earn was forded by a Roman road which ran from the fort at Braco (see Tour 14) towards Perth. The road, which is lined with a number of signal stations, was probably built during the invasion by Agricola in AD 83–84. **Return to the B8062 and turn right. Cross the River Earn at Kinkell Bridge and turn right immediately after it. Turn right at a T-junction towards Muthill D.** As you approach the little village of Muthill (pronounced

• PLACES OF INTEREST •

Crieff
In the eighteenth century Crieff was the site of Scotland's largest tryst, or annual cattle market. Farmers from all over the Highlands, and as far away as the Hebrides, would converge on Crieff with their herds in October, to do business with buyers from the Lowlands. Up to 30,000 head of cattle would change hands, and there would be much drinking and merrymaking in the town. The tryst was moved to Stenhousemuir in the 1770s, and during the nineteenth century Crieff developed into a fashionable Victorian resort. There are many good walks, and the surrounding scenery is superb, especially in autumn when the woods of Monzievaird to the west are a riot of red and gold.
Drummond Castle Gardens, 3 miles south of Crieff, is Scotland's largest formal garden, a series of parterres laid out in the shape of a St Andrews cross, with fountains, terraces, topiary and a remarkable sundial dating from 1630. Open May–October, daily 2–6. Telephone: (01764) 681257.
Innerpeffray Library. 4 miles southeast of Crieff. Open

daily 10–12.45 and 2–4.45, except Thursdays; Sundays 2–4. Closes at 4 October–March. Telephone: (01764) 652819.

Auchterarder
Known as 'The Lang Toon', Auchterarder extends along its one mile long main street on a low ridge beneath the steep northern scarp of the Ochil Hills. It was laid waste by the Earl of Mar following the Jacobite defeat at Sheriffmuir in 1715, and subsequently made a living from weaving and wool. The town played an important part in Scottish church history: the 'Auchterarder Creed' led to the creation of the Secession Church in 1732, and it was the actions of the Auchterarder presbytery that resulted in the Disruption of 1843, and the consequent founding of the Free Church of Scotland. Glenruthven Weaving Mill, on the east edge of town, houses a working steam textile engine, and an exhibition on the town's weaving industry, as well as a pottery and a bottlemaking workshop. There are many shops in the town selling antiques and woollen goods, and several pubs and tearooms.

'Mewthil'), you see the red sandstone tower of its parish church on the right. But the village is famous for its old parish church, which lies a little further on. Its square Romanesque tower dates from the twelfth century, and the ruined nave is fifteenth-century. Inside are the tombs of a local nobleman, Sir Muriel Drummond (died 1362), and his wife. **Turn left at the T-junction in Muthill, on the A823 towards Auchterarder. In a mile or so you have to turn left to stay on the A823. After another 2½ miles a sign on the left shows the way to Tullibardine Chapel, visible amid a small stand of pine trees.** This stretch of the A823 offers a fine view over the rich farmland of lower Strathearn. Tullibardine Chapel escaped the destruction that was wrought on many Scottish churches during the Reformation, and stands as a rare example of an unaltered fifteenth-century rural church. It has a fine wooden ceiling and stone carvings of the arms of its founding family, the Murrays, Earls of Atholl. **A mile beyond**

Tullibardine turn left onto the A824 into Auchterarder.

Go straight through Auchterarder, and on the far side of town turn right on the B8062 E to Dunning. The road follows the foot of the Ochil Hills, with a view across to the Gask ridge, along which runs the Roman road mentioned above. The attractive village of Dunning boasts the fine medieval Church of St Serf, which has a Romanesque tower dating from around 1210, similar to the one at Muthill. **In Dunning, go past the old church and turn left onto the B934 towards Forteviot and Perth.** Forteviot was the site of the Pictish capital in the centuries following the Roman invasions, and it was here that Kenneth MacAlpin, the king who first united the Scots and Pictish thrones in 843, died. **After about 2½ miles the route bends sharp left across a level crossing, crosses the River Earn and turns right onto the B9112.** On the hill to the left of the road the Battle of Dupplin Moor was fought in 1332. Here Edward Balliol, with the support

Muthill Old Church

of the English, wrested the Scottish throne from the 8-year-old David II, the son of Robert the Bruce, by defeating the forces of the regent Earl of Mar. To the right there is a good view of the River Earn meandering through the fields and woods of its fertile flood plain. **The road eventually passes beneath the M90 at the edge of Perth, then meets Glasgow Road. Turn right to return to Perth town centre.** ■

Perth

ABERFELDY, GLEN LYON, BEN LAWERS AND LOCH TAY

58 MILES – 3 HOURS
START AND FINISH IN ABERFELDY

Ben Lawers is Perthshire's highest peak, and its shapely summit supports a wealth of alpine plants unique in the British Isles. This route makes a circuit of the mountain, beginning in the thriving tourist town of Aberfeldy and heading up the beautiful valley of Glen Lyon. After stopping at the Ben Lawers Visitor Centre, from which experienced hillwalkers can climb to the summit, the route descends to Killin and the lovely Falls of Dochart, before returning along the southern shore of Loch Tay. Choose a fine day to make this tour, as the scenery is some of the finest in the country. In winter, the road over Ben Lawers is often closed by snow.

Pass the watermill in the middle of Aberfeldy's main street, then turn right on the B846 to Kinloch Rannoch. The route crosses the River Tay on Wade's Bridge, designed by William Adam and built by General Wade and his men between 1733 and 1735. General George Wade was a soldier and roadbuilder who played a major part in the pacification of the Highland clans by building a network of military roads and bridges, the first made roads ever seen in the region.

After passing through the little village of Weem, you will see Castle Menzies to the right. The castle, a fine example of a sixteenth-century Z-plan tower

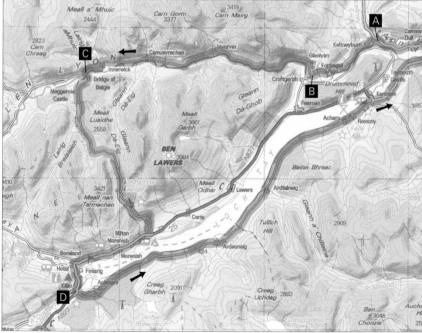

SCALE 1:250 000 OR 1 INCH TO 4 MILES *1 CM TO 2.5 KM*

Aberfeldy

Robert Burns immortalised *The Birks of Aberfeldy* in verse in 1787, and ever since then visitors have followed in his footsteps to enjoy the scenic splendours of this small highland town. If wet weather deters you from taking a walk through the birks (Scots for silver birches) to see the Falls of Moness, you can see oatmeal being made at the Aberfeldy Water Mill, or take a tour of the Aberfeldy Distillery, opened by John and Thomas Dewar in 1898. Beside General Wade's bridge over the

River Tay is a tall cairn topped by the figure of a kilted soldier. This is the Black Watch Memorial, which commemorates the first raising of the Black Watch regiment here in 1739.

Aberfeldy Water Mill. Open Easter–October, Monday–Saturday 10–5.30, Sunday 12–5.30. Telephone: (01887) 820803.

Aberfeldy Distillery. Guided tours and whisky testing. Open Monday–Friday 9.30–4.30 (restricted hours in winter – check by phone). Telephone: (01887) 820330.

house, has been the seat of the chiefs of Clan Menzies for over 400 years, and now houses a clan museum. The fifteenth-century church at Weem houses the Menzies family mausoleum. The road continues along the broad valley of the Tay, a historic area known as the Appin of Dull. The village of Camserney has several thatched cottages, and Dull itself was the site of a very early monastery founded by St Adamnan (the seventh-century

abbot of Iona who wrote the Life of St Columba). The floor of the glen is dotted with prehistoric cairns and stone circles.

About 5¹/₂ miles out of Aberfeldy, turn left at the Coshieville Hotel A towards Fortingall and Glen Lyon. The lower part of Glen Lyon is broad and flat-floored, its slopes covered in a mix of coniferous and deciduous woodland. **At Fortingall, turn off the road at the hotel to visit the kirkyard.** The church here contains a font and a bell that are said to have been used by St Adamnan, and in the kirkyard is a bushy and venerable yew tree that is reputedly around 3,000 years old, perhaps the oldest tree in Europe. The area certainly has a long history, as the standing stones and tumuli beside the river attest. There is even a local legend that claims that Pontius Pilate was born here, the son of a Roman envoy and a local girl. The lovely thatched cottages in the village were built around 1900 for the employees of the Glenlyon Estate. **Soon after leaving Fortingall, turn right on the road signposted Glen Lyon B.**

One of the longest and loveliest of Scotland's glens, Glen Lyon runs for 33 miles from the wilds of Rannoch Moor to the meadows of Aberfeldy. As one of the main overland routes between

Highlands and Lowlands, the glen has a long history of habitation, and the floor is strewn with the remains of abandoned homesteads. It is believed that St Adamnan, the ninth abbot of Iona, lived out his last years here at a mill near Bridge of Balgie. The glen is particularly associated with the sixteenth-century feud between the Campbells and the MacGregors. As the road winds along the valley, fine prospects of hills and forest open up, inviting you to stop and enjoy the view. But the single track road has few stopping places and you should press on to Innerwick where there is a car park and picnic area, or to the tearoom at Bridge of Balgie post office. **At Bridge of Balgie C, 11 miles from Fortingall, turn left across the river towards the Ben Lawers Visitor Centre.**

A bridge to the right of the road, a half mile out of Bridge of Balgie, leads to a house called Milton Eonan, which is thought to be the site of Adamnan's mill. The road now climbs up the attractive glen of the Allt Bail a' Mhuillin (Stream of the Mill Village) and, once you leave the forestry plantation behind, the view opens up with the shoulder of Ben Lawers rising high on your left. The burn cascades over a series of little waterfalls and there are many appealing picnic spots, but

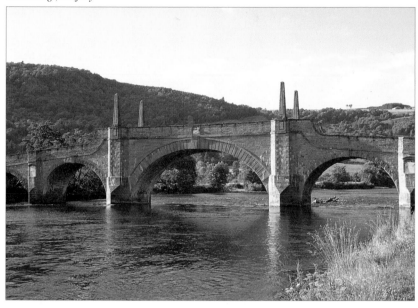

• PLACES OF INTEREST •

Ben Lawers

With a height of 3,984 feet (1,215m), Ben Lawers is one of Scotland's loftiest mountains. The mountain's combination of high altitude and lime-bearing bedrock has allowed a unique alpine flora to develop, including alpine forget-me-not, snow gentian and saxifrage, an assemblage of plants found nowhere else in Britain. The importance of the site prompted the National Trust for Scotland to acquire 8,000 acres (3,237 hectares) of the mountain in 1950, and the Nature Conservancy Council added another 11,000 acres (4,452 hectares) in 1975 to create the Ben Lawers National Nature Reserve.

The visitor centre contains imaginative exhibits describing the geology, botany and wildlife of the mountain, and provides a ranger service should you need advice on walks or further information on natural history. Above the car park there is a short nature trail (about 1 1/2 miles) that loops through a fenced-in reserve on either side of the Edramucky Burn and which you can explore with a self-guided tour leaflet. The footpath to the summit (a 6-mile round trip with 2,000 feet of ascent) should only be attempted by experienced and fully-equipped hillwalkers. The views from the summit are superb, ranging from Ben Lomond in the south to Ben Nevis and the Cairngorms. On a clear day you might even make out the Paps of Jura, 80 miles away to the southwest.

Visitor Centre open Good Friday–September, daily 10–5.

Loch Tay

At 15 miles long, and averaging almost a mile wide, Loch Tay is the sixth largest of Scotland's lochs. Though less famous than Loch Ness, and lacking a monster, it is certainly one of the country's most scenic lochs, with a fringe of wooded shores trailing beneath a backdrop of high mountains. It is fed at the west end by the rivers Dochart and Lochay, and drained at the east by the Tay, Scotland's longest river (120 miles, 193km if measured from the source of one of its headwaters on the slopes of Ben Lui to the mouth of the firth at Dundee), and one of its famous salmon streams.

again few suitable stopping places. The road passes through an area of old shielings (marked on the OS Landranger map) of which little is visible today except for the occasional low stone wall. These were the temporary dwellings used by the old Highland cattle farmers when they took their cows up to the high pastures for the summer. Their remains can be found in many of the high corries around Glen Lyon and Loch Tay.

As the road reaches the crest of the pass at a height of over 1,800 feet you are rewarded with a grand view of Lochan na Lairige, a sheet of crumpled silver beneath the dark shoulder of Meall nan Tarmachan. Like many lochs in the area, it has been dammed for hydroelectric power, the outflow being taken by pipeline to the Finlarig power station near Killin. **About a mile beyond the Lochan na Lairige dam pull into the Ben Lawers Visitor Centre car park on the left.**

Continue downhill. At the foot of the hill the road forks; go right, then turn right on the A827 towards Killin. The pretty tourist resort of Killin sits beside the Falls of Dochart, probably the most photographed, most painted and most gazed at waterfall in Scotland – the bridge carrying the main road makes an excellent viewpoint. More of a white-water spectacle than a true cascade, the River Dochart plunges and boils over a series of rocky slabs and ledges before emptying into Loch Tay. Killin has long been associated with Clan Macnab, who claim descent from the ninth-century abbot of Glendochart, son of Kenneth MacAlpin. Inchbuie, the little island in the river downstream from the bridge, was for centuries the Macnab burial ground. To visit the island, which is reached via a gate, ask for the key from the tourist information office in Killin.

Go through Killin and cross the bridge below the Falls of Dochart, then turn left almost immediately, signposted Achmore **D**. If you want to stop to admire the falls, there is a parking space about 200 yards upstream on the main road. The narrow road along the south shore of Loch Tay offers a constantly changing vista of mountains, woods and waters, and there are a few parking spots where you can stop to admire the scenery. Towards the north end of

Fortingall

the loch, at Acharn, a short and easy walk (a round trip of 1 mile) leads uphill from the road to the Hermitage Cave, which leads to a rock ledge overlooking the Falls of Acharn.

The route rejoins the A827 at the north end of the loch. Turn left to visit Kenmore village. Kenmore enjoys the reputation of being Scotland's prettiest village, set on a hillock overlooking the north end of the loch. It was built as a model village in 1779 by the third Earl of Breadalbane, to house the people who worked his estate. The

picturesque church and rustic cottages sit between a bridge over the Tay, built in 1774, and the huge Gothic gateway to Taymouth Castle, the seat of the Earls and Marquises of Breadalbane. Robert Burns visited the hotel beside the church during his Highland tour of 1787, and wrote some verses in pencil on the chimney breast to commemorate his visit. Taymouth Castle, once the grandest of Scottish stately homes and host to Queen Victoria in 1842, was sold by the family in 1922 and now lies empty. **Return along the A827 to Aberfeldy.** ■

Lawers Dam, Lochan na Lairige

THE FIRTH OF TAY

57 MILES – 2¹/₂ HOURS
START AND FINISH IN PERTH

The Firth of Tay stretches for 18 miles from Perth to Dundee, with fertile farmland backed by steep hills lining its shores. This tour follows the southern shore of the firth, past pretty villages and ruined abbeys, before crossing to the north side via the Tay Road Bridge. From the lively city of Dundee, the route then heads back through the berry fields of the Carse of Gowrie, to finish on the summit of Kinnoull Hill, from where you can enjoy a magnificent panoramic view back over the ground you have just explored.

Leave Perth city centre heading south on the A912 towards junction 10 on the M90. At a bus stop just before you reach the junction, turn left on a minor road signposted Rhynd . Off to the left you have a view across the River Tay to the steep, wooded crags of Kinnoull Hill. Soon you can see the churchtower of Rhynd ahead. **Just beyond the hamlet of Rhynd, turn left to visit Elcho Castle.** The narrow track leads downhill through a farm to a parking area beside the castle, which sits on a rise above the River Tay. **Return to the main road and turn left.**

Beyond Rhynd the road runs downhill to the flat plain of the River Earn, with a grand prospect of the Firth of Tay ahead. **When you see a 'No Through Road' sign ahead turn sharp right. After passing under the M90, turn left through Bridge of Earn, and continue on the A912 towards Newburgh. At a roundabout 2¹/₂ miles after Bridge of Earn go left towards Abernethy on the A913. As you enter Abernethy, turn right at a prominent white fence (signpost for Abernethy**

Round Tower hidden in foliage), then right again at The Corner Shop, to a parking area at Mercat Cross. It was here that King Malcolm Canmore met and made peace with William the Conqueror in 1072. The village was once the capital of a Pictish kingdom, and later supported an Augustinian monastery, but today it is famous for the late eleventh-century Round Tower that overlooks the Mercat Cross. The tower is one of only two left in Scotland (the

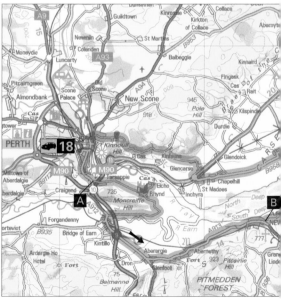

Pictish stone at Abernethy

SCALE 1:250 000 OR 1 INCH TO 4 MILES *1 CM TO 2.5 KM*

Elcho Castle

This fine multi-towered castle was built for the Wemyss family between the fourteenth and the sixteenth centuries, and is still in their possession (though now cared for by Historic Scotland). It has four projecting towers, two round and two square, complete with original wrought iron grilles protecting the windows. The remains of an old stone quay can be seen on the bank of a small inlet below the castle. You can't get into the castle itself, but the grounds are open all year.

other is in Brechin), but there are 80 in Ireland. They were associated with early Christian churches, and probably served the dual purpose of lookout tower and place of refuge. A Pictish symbol stone lies at the foot of the 74-foot tall structure.

Continue past the Mercat Cross to the main road and turn right. Newburgh once made a living from weaving and linoleum manufacture, and is still a lively little town today. **Go through Newburgh, and turn left at the Abbey Garage service station B, signposted**

Wormit. About a hundred yards beyond the junction, in a low-walled enclosure on the left, lie the overgrown, pink sandstone ruins of Lindores Abbey. Founded in 1191, this was once one of Scotland's most important religious communities, but following its sacking by Reformers in the sixteenth century it fell into disrepair and was used as a quarry by local folk.

The road now runs along a hillside with grand views across the Firth which at low tide exposes a maze of treacherous mud and sandbanks. The

prominent tower belongs to Ballinbreich Castle where Mary Queen of Scots once stayed during a visit to Fife. **Six and a half miles from Newburgh, when you reach the crossroads at Hazelton Walls C, turn left. After another 1½ miles, turn left again towards Balmerino. After a further half mile, just past some white cottages, turn left to visit Balmerino Abbey (blue National Trust for Scotland sign).** The Cistercian abbey was founded about 1227 as a daughter house of Melrose Abbey in the Borders (see Tour 6), but was burned by English invaders in 1547 and sacked by Reformers in 1559. A few Gothic vaults remain in the Chapter House, and there are picnic tables within the abbey precinct. A ferry once crossed the Firth from an old pier below the pretty cottages next to the abbey, carrying pilgrims on their way to Arbroath. Dundee is visible across the water, sprawled below the conical outline of Dundee Law. **Return to the main road and after 2½ miles, at a T-junction with the B946, turn left into Wormit, and on through Newport-on-Tay.** Wormit is the southern terminus of the two-mile long Tay Railway Bridge, built between 1883 and 1888. Just to the east of the bridge you can see the stumps of its

predecessor which opened in 1877 but collapsed during a storm on 28 December 1879. Tragically, a train was on the bridge at the time, and 75 people perished in the icy waters of the Tay, an event immortalised in a famously bad poem by the notorious William MacGonagall. There is a good walk along the coast from Wormit to Balmerino (3 miles one-way).

Wormit merges into Newport-on-Tay, whose grand nineteenth-century villas were built by the wealthy 'jute barons' of Dundee. One of the oldest ferry crossings in Scotland – from Tayport to Broughty Ferry – lies 3 miles to the east; boats have plied these waters regularly since at least the twelfth century. The Newport to Dundee ferry began service in 1822, and continued until 1966 when the Tay Road Bridge was opened. The bridge is 1 1/2 miles long, and its 42 spans carry the roadway 120 feet above the water. **Pass under the south end of the Tay Road Bridge, and turn right to cross the bridge to Dundee. At the far end of the bridge get into the lefthand lane, and follow signs for Discovery Point.** There is a large car park here, should you wish to visit Discovery Point and Dundee's other attractions.

Continue past Discovery Point on the A85 towards

Perth. Pass the airport, and soon after crossing a bridge over the railway turn left into Invergowrie. Turn left at the church onto Errol Road. The return leg of this route passes through the Carse of Gowrie. The word carse comes from the Norse for 'marsh', and indeed much of this flat, low-lying area has been reclaimed from the marshes north of the Firth of Tay. It has always been a fertile area and is now given over largely to fruit growing. In centuries past the land was owned by noble families whose castles can be seen dotted about the flats. As you negotiate a level crossing, Castle Huntly can be seen off to the right. It was built

in the fifteenth century for Lord Gray of Fowlis Easter but now serves as a young offenders institution. **Turn left at a T-junction towards Errol.** You go through the village of Grange and pass, to the left of the road, an old aerodrome, now home to a skydiving club. **A right turn at the next T-junction leads in half a mile to a level crossing and Errol Station Railway Heritage Centre.** Here, on the main Perth to Dundee line, is an original station building of 1847, complete with ticket office, waiting rooms (separate ladies and gents) and porter's house, restored as they would have appeared in the 1920s. There is a

River Tay from Kinnoull Hill

refreshment room and a museum of historical railway items. Megginch Castle, seat of the Drummond family, lies behind the band of trees to the west of the road beyond the railway. To reach the entrance continue along the B958 to the A90 and go left for almost a mile. The castle gardens are open to the public, and contain a sixteenth-century rose garden, an eighteenth-century physic garden, and several 1,000-year-old yew trees.

Return along the B958 into Errol. At the far end of the village turn left in front of a grand gatehouse D **towards St Madoes.** This last section of the B958 runs along the crest of a low ridge, with views of the firth to the south, and the steep scarp of the Braes of the Carse to the north. **Cross the bridge over the A90 at St Madoes and turn right through Glencarse village. Pass the hotel and go left towards Kinfauns.** The road runs through the pretty little valley of Glen Carse, with flat meadows and steep wooded crags. **After 2 miles, at some cottages on the right, turn right, signposted Kinnoull.** These woods are the haunt of the elusive red squirrel and a concerned resident has erected a novel road sign on the steep hill here: 'Caution: red squirrels

crossing'! The narrow road winds along a steep hillside with grand views of the Tay below and Kinnoull Hill up ahead. **At the top of the hill is the Jubilee car park on the right.** This car park is the starting point for many good walks on Kinnoull Hill. **The road continues past the car park and runs downhill into Perth city centre at the old bridge.** ■

• PLACES OF INTEREST •

Dundee
Dundee is a bustling, modern industrial and commercial city with a population of about 166,000. It spreads beneath the slopes of Dundee Law (570 feet, 174m) whose summit is capped by an Iron Age fort – Dun Diagh – which may have given the city its name. It is known as the city of 'jute, jam and journalism', a reference to the three industries that once provided most of the city's employment: the spinning and weaving of jute yarn, the bottling of fruit from the surrounding farms, and D.C. Thomson's newspaper and magazine publishing empire. The demand for vessels to carry jute from India to Britain led to the development of Dundee's other great industry, shipbuilding. The shipyards lining the Tay produced many famous vessels, including the RRS *Discovery*, which carried Captain Scott's 1901–04 expedition to the Antarctic.

Discovery Point, near the north end of the Tay Road Bridge, is a special dry dock and exhibition complex where the original *Discovery* is now permanently berthed. The exhibition leads you through the ship's design and construction, Scott's expedition and the ship's subsequent history. Afterwards you can go on board *Discovery* and explore her for yourself, including the atmospheric wardroom and the restored cabins of Scott and his officers.

Open Monday–Saturday 10–5 (last admission), Sunday 11–5; November–March, last admission at 4. Telephone: (01382) 201245.

Verdant Works, 27 West Henderson's Wynd. A typical nineteenth-century jute mill that now serves as a living museum of Dundee's textile industry. Open June–August, Monday–Friday 12–5. Telephone: (01382) 26659.

Barrack Street Museum, in the city centre, houses a collection covering local history, and Scottish geology and natural history. Open Monday–Saturday 10–5. Telephone: (01382) 23141 ext 65162.

Errol Station Railway Heritage Centre. Open May–September, Sundays only 12–5. Telephone: (015754) 222.

Perth
Known as 'The Fair City', Perth enjoys a beautiful setting on the banks of the River Tay. Once an important trading port and cattle market, it is still famous today for its annual Bull Sales. The town centre is clustered around historic St John's Kirk, where a hellfire sermon preached by John Knox in 1559 marked the beginning of the Reformation. Nearby, the Tay is spanned by the nine arches of the Old Perth Bridge, built in 1771 and still going strong. The attractive parkland of the North Inch borders the river upstream from the bridge, where Balhousie Castle provides a home for the Black Watch Regimental Museum. The steep, wooded crags of Kinnoull Hill (729 ft/222m) rise to the south-east of Perth, providing a panoramic view of the Firth of Tay. A 15-minute walk from the Jubilee car park leads through pleasant woods to Kinnoull Tower, a circular stone turret perched precariously on the edge of a high cliff.

Branklyn Garden, at the foot of Kinnoull Hill, has an impressive collection of rare and unusual plants, including the beautiful Himalayan blue poppy. Open 1 March–31 October, daily 9.30–sunset. Telephone: (01738) 625535.

SCONE, BLAIRGOWRIE, PITLOCHRY AND DUNKELD

70 MILES – 3 HOURS
START AND FINISH IN PERTH

Scone, the ancient crowning place of Scottish kings, is the first stop on this lengthy tour into the historic Highland fringe. From here the tour heads north, by way of the berry fields of Blairgowrie, to the scenic glen of Strathardle, which penetrates deep into the foothills of the Highlands. After climbing over the pass beneath Ben Vuirich, the route drops down to the tourist town of Pitlochry, then heads back south along lovely Strath Tay, where you can explore the delightful village of Dunkeld. This route is not recommended in winter, when deep snow can block the road between Strathardle and Pitlochry.

Cross the Tay at the old bridge and turn left. Bear left at the traffic lights on the A93 (follow signs for Blairgowrie and Braemar). After 1 mile you come to the entrance to Scone Palace on the left. The short driveway leads to a car park where you can buy your ticket and walk up to the palace. **Return to the main road and continue north on the A93 for 15 miles to Blairgowrie.** The road runs through the rich farmland of lower Strath Tay with many of the fields devoted to the raspberries for which the area is famous. At Meikleour (pronounced

M'Cloor), 11 miles from Scone, the road runs alongside a huge beech hedge. The hedge was planted in 1746 and is now 580 yards long and 100 feet high, earning it an entry in the *Guinness Book of Records* as the highest of its kind in the world. For the gardeners who maintain it, it is the hedge-clipping equivalent of painting the Forth Bridge! **When you arrive in Blairgowrie turn right at the traffic lights beside the garden square in the town centre, and then right again to park in front of the tourist information office.**

Blairgowrie is the raspberry capital of Scotland, lying at the centre of the world's leading raspberry growing area. The fruit plants flourish in the mild climate on the predominantly south-facing slopes. During the summer the region sees a huge influx of temporary workers who combine a holiday in the country with the chance to make a little money picking the berries. The town is now a popular touring base for visitors, but in the nineteenth century it earned a living from the spinning of flax and jute, using the power of the River Ericht to turn the great mill wheels. One of the old jute mills at Keathbank, on the northern edge of town, is being restored as a Heritage Centre. **From the tourist office turn right, then left at the traffic lights and cross the bridge over the River Ericht. Take the third street on the left after the bridge, turning onto the A93 towards Braemar. About a mile along this road is the entrance to Keathbank Mill.** The route continues up the valley of the River Ericht, a fast-flowing Highland stream famous for its salmon. **At Bridge of**

Scone Palace

Cally, cross the bridge and turn left at the post office onto the A924 to Pitlochry.

The road now enters the long valley of Strathardle, which cuts deep into the Highland foothills. This fertile glen has long been a centre of habitation and the hills to either side are scattered with the remains of old farming settlements and field systems. Modern farmers continue to take advantage of the rich alluvial soil of the valley floor and in summer the glen is golden with fields of hay. The scenery becomes grander as you pass beyond the hamlet of Kirkmichael and the shapely peak of Ben Vuirich rises ahead. At Enochdhu a minor road on the left leads to Kindrogan Field Centre where you can explore a nature trail or climb to the viewpoint on the summit of

87

Perth
For information, see Tour 18

Scone Palace
Scone (pronounced 'Scoon') is one of Scotland's most sacred sites, long hallowed as the place where Scottish kings were crowned. Kenneth MacAlpin made it his capital after uniting the Scots and Pictish kingdoms around AD 840, bringing with him the Stone of Destiny on which each new king was enthroned. The stone was stolen by Edward I of England in 1296 and has never been returned – it is beneath the Coronation Throne in Westminster Abbey.

The site of the ancient abbey is now occupied by Scone Palace, the neo-Gothic home of the Earls of Mansfield, built in 1802. The palace contains a fine collection of period furniture, porcelain, ivory and family memorabilia. Open Good Friday–mid October, Monday–Saturday 9.30–5, Sunday 1.30–5 (10–5 July and August). Telephone: (01738) 52300.

Keathbank Mill
An old jute mill, built in 1864 on the banks of the River Ericht at Blairgowrie. It is being restored and currently offers an unusual blend of attractions. First comes a

heraldry museum and workshop, then a tour of the old mill, with a chance to see Scotland's second-largest working waterwheel, and finally one of Britain's largest model railway layouts. Open April–October, daily 10–6. Telephone: (01250) 872025.

Edradour Distillery
Scotland's smallest and most picturesque distillery, established in 1825, nestles in a fold of the hills above Pitlochry. Open March–October, Monday–Saturday 9.30–5; November–February 10.30–4. Telephone: (01796) 472095.

Kindrogan Hill. At Straloch the glen sweeps round to the west and the hayfields give way to hill sheep as the road climbs over the pass to Pitlochry, at a height of 1,260 feet (384m).

Twenty miles beyond Bridge of Cally, the road descends towards Pitlochry. Where it makes a sharp right turn, go left to visit Edradour Distillery . Otherwise continue downhill into Pitlochry. At the T-junction, turn left along the main street to reach the car park beside

Edradour Distillery

the tourist information office.
Turn left out of the car park, pass beneath the arched railway bridge, and turn right on Bridge Road (signpost for Clunymore and Logierait) B. Pass a caravan site and turn left towards Dunfallandy (single track road). On the right of the road, just after it passes beneath a bridge, is a track leading to the Dunfallandy Stone, a 1,000-year-old Pictish sculpted stone with a Celtic cross on one side and animal figures on the other. **After 4 miles the route descends steeply to the Logierait Hotel and turns left onto the A827, before joining the A9. Turn left towards Perth. Watch out for a signpost for Dowally on the left. Pass this, and a half mile later turn left C on the A923 to Blairgowrie.** This two-lane road is the old A9, now superseded by the modern highway below. It climbs through the forest, and bends left beneath the steep, rocky crags of Craig a Barns, a favourite haunt of rock climbers. **After passing a small lily-covered loch on the left, turn left D on the A923 Blairgowrie road to visit Loch of the Lowes Nature Reserve.** One mile from the junction turn right on a minor road to reach a

car park, from which a footpath leads through the woods to the Scottish Wildlife Trust's Visitor Centre. The loch is famed as a nesting site for ospreys, and you can watch these majestic birds from the centre's special hide (binoculars provided). They lay their eggs in early May and you can expect to see young birds in the nest in June and July. The centre explains the loch's ecology and describes the birdlife you can expect to see.

The main route continues straight on into Dunkeld. Towards the end of the High Street turn right into the village square and park at The Cross. There is a tourist information office and a National Trust shop in the square. **Turn right out of Dunkeld's main square towards the river, but then turn left onto the A984 immediately before the bridge, towards Coupar Angus.** The route runs through wooded hills above the river, roughly following the line of General Wade's old military road. **After 4 miles, at Caputh, turn right on the B9099 towards Stanley.** The village of Stanley was built in 1785 as a model mill town, inspired by the success of David Dale's experiment at New Lanark (see Tour 3). The cotton-

spinning mill, powered by the waters of the Tay, provided employment for 1,200 workers in the nineteenth century, who were housed in the specially built tenements and terraces near to the factory, complete with village school and church. **Continue on this road to Luncarty.** Luncarty was the site of a great victory in 990 for the army of the Scots king Kenneth II over the invading Norsemen. Legend has it that a Viking soldier, creeping up on the Scottish camp during the night, trod on a thistle and let out a yell, alerting the Scots to the presence of their attackers. For this reason the thistle was adopted as a Scottish emblem (this story is also applied to the Battle of Largs in 1263). **On leaving Luncarty turn left onto the A9, which leads back to Perth.** ∎

• PLACES OF INTEREST •

Pitlochry
Situated in the geographical heart of Scotland, Pitlochry has been a thriving tourist town since Queen Victoria passed through in 1844. Its tidy streets of Victorian villas, set along the banks of the River Tummel, contain more holiday accommodation than any other town of its size in the country. Pitlochry's best-known attraction is the Loch Faskally Dam and Power Station, where a glass-fronted chamber lets visitors watch the salmon swimming up the fish ladder. It is also home to the world-famous Pitlochry Festival Theatre, which stages a summer-long season of plays and concerts. There are many fine walks in the area, especially around Loch Faskally and at the Pass of Killiecrankie, three miles to the north.

Loch of the Lowes Visitor Centre
Nature reserve with birdwatching hide (the hide is wheelchair accessible). Open April–September, daily 10–5 (6 in July and August). Telephone: (01350) 727337.

Dunkeld
The village of Dunkeld was completely rebuilt following its destruction by warring Highlanders and Covenanters in the aftermath of Killiecrankie in 1689. The 'Little Houses', clustered around The Cross, have been restored by the NTS, and make for an exceptionally pretty village square. Dunkeld, meaning 'Fort of the Celts', is an ancient religious settlement, the site of a monastery founded in the sixth century by St Columba, and the joint Scottish capital (with Scone) under Kenneth MacAlpin in the ninth century. Dunkeld Cathedral, half-ruined and romantic, rises among the trees on a lovely greensward beside the Tay. Wrecked by Reformers in 1560, the elegant fifteenth-century Gothic nave and tower stand roofless, but the choir was repaired in the nineteenth century and now serves as the parish kirk.

There are many lovely walks in the vicinity of Dunkeld, along the banks of the Tay and its tributary the Braan. On the far bank of the Tay, spanned by Telford's graceful bridge of 1809, is the village of Birnam. On the river bank is the massive Birnam Oak, its huge limbs supported on crutches, which is said to be a survivor of the original Birnam Wood mentioned in Shakespeare's *Macbeth*. Dunsinane Hill, the site of Macbeth's fort, lies 12 miles to the south-east.

DUNDEE, ARBROATH, BRECHIN AND GLAMIS CASTLE

74 MILES – 3½ HOURS
START AND FINISH IN DUNDEE

The region to the northeast of Dundee was a centre for early Christianity and this tour takes you to the three major religious sites of Arbroath, Brechin and Restenneth. Before the arrival of Christianity this was a Pictish kingdom and the art of these early inhabitants is preserved in the mysterious sculpted stones at Aberlemno. The return leg of the tour takes in the splendid stately home of Glamis Castle. There are good beaches and picnic sites on the first part of the route between Carnoustie and Montrose.

From the junction at the north end of the Tay Road Bridge take the A92 (signposted Arbroath and Montrose) past the docks. After 1 mile the A92 veers left, but keep straight on, on the A930 towards Broughty Ferry. After 3 miles look out for West Ferry post office on the right. Just beyond the pedestrian crossing at the post office, turn first right down Douglas Terrace **A**. This road runs along the seafront to the recently renovated harbour beside the grim sixteenth-century fortress of Broughty Castle. For many years a ferry plied the waters between here and Tayport, one mile away to the south. The history of the ferries, and of the local fishing and whaling industries, is recorded in the castle's museum. Good sandy beaches stretch eastwards from

here to Monifieth.

Turn left at the pier opposite the castle, along St Vincent Street. Pass under a railway bridge and turn right at the traffic lights. Continue through Monifieth on the A930 to Carnoustie. Just before Carnoustie, a blue NTS signpost points down a minor road on the left to Barry Mill. Here a working watermill sits on the Pitairlie Burn, and visitors can watch the entire milling process from the grinding of the oats to the bagging of the meal. A walkway leads along the mill-lade to a picnic area in an apple orchard. Carnoustie itself is famous for its golfcourses, set in the sandy links to the south of the town, where many important tournaments are played. In Carnoustie, where the main road bends sharp left, go straight on towards East Haven. The road runs along

a stretch of rocky coast to the tiny sandy beach and picnic area at East Haven where small fishing boats are drawn up on the shore. The buoys of the fishermen's lobster pots can be seen bouncing in the waves just offshore. Go left in East Haven, back to the A92, where you turn right towards Arbroath.

Follow A92 Montrose road out of Arbroath. On the edge of town, at the Meadowbank Inn, turn right towards Seaton and Auchmithie **B**. Turn left at a T-junction. After a half mile turn right to visit Auchmithie. This is a picturesque little fishing village perched on top of a rocky inlet in the cliffs, with a pub and some

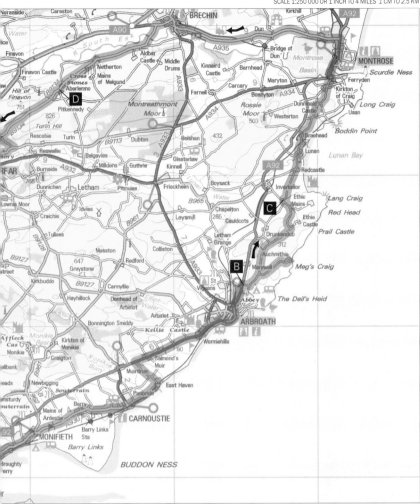

pleasant coastal walking. **Four miles beyond the Auchmithie turning are two T-junctions in quick succession C; turn right at both, towards Lunan.** The road wends its way through rich farmland and down to the huge sandy beach of Lunan Bay, overlooked by the hollow red sandstone ruin of Red Castle. There is a parking area in Lunan village if you want to stop and visit the beach.

The road finally descends towards Montrose. Turn left to a roundabout, where you exit right to Montrose town centre. As you cross the bridge over the mouth of the South Esk River you can see Montrose Basin to the left – a sheet of silver water,

or an expanse of grey mud, depending on the state of the tide. The tidal lagoon is now a nature reserve – an important feeding ground for huge flocks of geese, waders and wildfowl. The town itself offers an interesting museum, a sandy beach and numerous tearooms. **About a mile past the tourist information office, turn left on the A935 to Brechin.** Here the route runs along the north shore of the basin and at low tide you can see the remains of medieval stone fish traps way out among the mudbanks. On the right is the entrance to the National Trust for Scotland's House of Dun. This magnificent Georgian mansion was built in

Pictish cross slab at Aberlemno Church

91

Brechin-Round Tower door

Dundee.
See Tour 18.
Broughty Castle Museum. Open all year, Monday–Saturday 10–1 and 2–5 (but closed Fridays); Sundays (July–September only). Telephone: (01382) 76121.
Barry Mill. Open Good Friday to 30 September, daily 11–5; October (until third Sunday), Saturdays and Sundays only 11–5. Telephone: (01241) 856761.

Arbroath
Originally known as Aberbrothock, this royal burgh secured its place in Scottish history in 1320 when Scotland's leaders met here and signed the Declaration of Arbroath, which asserted their country's independence of the English crown, and recognised Robert the Bruce as their king. Its stirring words, engraved on the memorial at Bannockburn (see Tour 12), foreshadow the American Declaration of Independence: 'For as long as one hundred of us shall remain alive we shall never in any wise consent to submit to the rule of the English, for it is not for glory we fight, for riches or for honours, but for freedom alone, which no good man loses but with his life.'
The document was signed at Arbroath Abbey which had been founded in 1178 by the Scottish king William the Lion. The red sandstone ruins of the abbey preserve many beautiful examples of the mason's art, notably the

magnificent circular window in the south transept where passages within the walls allow you to climb high into the stonework. The well-preserved Abbot's House contains a Gothic vaulted kitchen and a small museum.
There are two other museums in town that are worth visiting: Arbroath Museum, housed in the former Signal Tower near the harbour, illustrates the flax, fishing and engineering industries which earned the town its living in the more recent past; and the St Vigil's Museum, a collection of Pictish gravestones housed in a little cottage on the northern edge of town.
Modern Arbroath is a popular holiday resort with beaches to the south and a busy harbour. There is a scenic nature trail along the cliffs to the north of town.
Arbroath Abbey. Open April–September, 9.30–6.30 Monday–Saturday, 2–6.30 Sundays; October–March, 9.30–4.30 Monday–Saturday, 2–4.30 Sundays. Telephone: (01241) 78756.
Arbroath Museum. Open 10–5 Monday–Saturday. Telephone: (01241) 75598.
House of Dun. Walled garden, woodland walks, shop and restaurant. Open Good Friday–30 June and 1–30 September, 1.30–5.30 daily; July and August, 11–5.30 daily; October (until third Sunday), 1.30–5.30 Saturdays and Sundays only. Telephone: (01674) 810264.

Aberlemno, at the foot of a hill, turn left **E** on a narrow road signposted Myreside. Turn right at a T-junction onto the B9113. After half a mile turn right to visit Restenneth Priory. The priory was founded for the Augustinian order by David I in 1150, as a daughter house of Jedburgh Abbey, and was built on the site of an older church – the base of the tower dates from the eleventh century. The monks added the upper part of the tower in the twelfth century, and a long, narrow choir and nave to either side of it; the elegant, pointed spire was added in the fifteenth century. **Continue into Forfar town centre. Go straight ahead at traffic lights and along High Street.** The textile town of Forfar was once home to a castle where, in 1057, King Malcolm Canmore first conferred titles on the Scottish nobility. The site of the castle is marked by an octagonal stone turret. The town's history is explained in a nearby museum, housed in the public library, called the Meffan Institute. There are nature walks and a picnic area at Forfar Loch to the east of town. **Go straight ahead at lights at the far end of town on the A929 and continue across the A90 towards Coupar Angus. After 5 miles turn right into the village of Glamis.** In the village itself, with its picture-postcard cottages, you will find the Angus Folk Museum,

1730 by the famous Scottish architect William Adam and contains splendid ornamental plasterwork.
Leave Brechin on the A935 towards Forfar, but just after passing the entrance to Brechin Castle turn left on the B9134 to Aberlemno. There is a fine view to the right across the broad, fertile valley of Strathmore with the Highlands rising beyond. **At Aberlemno the road passes three carved Pictish stones on**

the lefthand verge; turn left after these **D** to visit Aberlemno church. There is a small parking place outside the church. The churchyard contains an eighth-century stone cross-slab, carved with a Celtic Christian cross on one side and a Pictish battle scene on the other. Walk back to the main road to look at the other stones; one bears a cross and a hunting scene, while the others show typical Pictish symbols. **Three miles beyond**

Claypotts Castle

Glamis Castle

housed in a nineteenth-century terrace. Inside is a collection of historic items which illustrate domestic and agricultural life in the region during the past 200 years. Just beyond the village is an ornamental gateway that opens onto a huge tree-lined avenue, almost a mile long, leading to Glamis Castle.

From Glamis take the A928 towards Dundee. The road climbs through a deep notch in the Sidlaw Hills called Lumley Den. **When you reach the A90 dual carriageway, turn right. Almost immediately, exit left at Petterden** ▉. **After a mile, at a crossroads, turn left.** The route now passes through rolling wheat fields to the north of Dundee, before turning south towards Broughty Ferry. **Turn left**

at a T-junction and right at the next, onto the B978 towards Broughty Ferry. Turn left onto a dual carriageway and keep in the righthand lane. Turn right, then at next set of traffic lights go left (look for a brown tourist sign for Claypotts Castle). On the right side of the road rises the distinctive outline of Claypotts Castle, with its quaint little

corbelled turrets jutting out of the corners. The castle was built in the sixteenth century for John Graham of Claverhouse (known in song and story as 'Bonnie Dundee') and is in a remarkably well-preserved state. It is not open to the public. **Continue past the castle along Claypotts Road. At traffic lights turn right to head back towards Dundee city centre.** ▪

• PLACES OF INTEREST •

Brechin
The cathedral city of Brechin is perhaps the smallest city in Scotland with a population of only 7,500. Brechin was granted its charter in 1150 when the cathedral was founded by King David I. The cathedral, perched above a wooded glen, underwent much rebuilding in the nineteenth century, but some thirteenth-century piers survive, and there are a few tenth- to thirteenth-century gravestones. The most distinctive feature, however, is the Round Tower, one of only two such

structures on the Scottish mainland (the other is in Abernethy, see Tour 18). Built by Irish masons between 990 and 1012, and capped with a fifteenth-century pointed roof, the tower stands hard against the cathedral like a factory chimney, its narrow door decorated with a carving of the crucifixion.

Glamis Castle
The original castle was granted to the Lyon family by Robert III in 1372 but its present appearance dates from the seventeenth century

when the Lyons became Earls of Strathmore. It is one of the most beautiful and romantic of Scottish castles with a magnificent interior which can be seen on one of the fascinating hour-long guided tours. The castle was the childhood home of Her Majesty Queen Elizabeth the Queen Mother, and the birthplace in 1930 of Her Royal Highness The Princess Margaret. There are extensive grounds, a restaurant and shop, and children's playground. Open April–October, daily 11–5. Telephone: (01307) 840242.

USEFUL ADDRESSES AND INFORMATION

National and Area Tourist Boards

Scottish Tourist Board
23 Ravelston Terrace,
Edinburgh EH3 4EU
Tel. (0131) 332 2433 (written and
telephone enquiries only).

Edinburgh and Lothians Tourist Board
4 Rothesay Terrace,
Edinburgh EH3 7RY
Tel: (0131) 226 6800

Argyll, The Isles, Loch Lomond, Stirling, Trossachs Tourist Board
41 Dunbarton Street,
Stirling FK8 2QQ
Tel: (01786) 470945

Angus and City of Dundee Tourist Board
4 City Square,
Dundee D1 3BA
Tel. 01382 434664

Perthshire Tourist Board
Lower City Mills,
West Mill Street,
Perth PH1 5QP
Tel: (01738) 627958

Scottish Borders Tourist Board
70 High Street,
Selkirk TD7 4DD
Tel: (01750) 20555

Kingdom of Fife Tourist Board
4 Market Street,
St Andrews KY16 9NU
Tel: (01334) 422021

Greater Glasgow and Clyde Valley Tourist Board
39 St Vincent Place,
Glasgow G1 2ER
Tel: (0141) 204 4400

Tourist Information Centres

(Only those marked * will respond to written enquiries)

Aberfeldy
The Square
Tel: (01877) 820276

*Arbroath
Market Place,
Arbroath DD11 1HR
Tel: (01241) 872609

Auchterarder
90 High Street
Tel: (01764) 664235

Blairgowrie
26 Wellmeadow
Tel: (01250) 872960/873701

Burntisland
4 Kirkgate
Tel: (01592) 872667

Crieff
Town Hall, High Street
Tel: (01764) 652578

Dalkeith
The Library,
White Hart Street
Tel: (0131) 663 2083/660 6818

Dunbar
143 High Street
Tel: (01368) 863353

*Dundee
4 City Square,
Dundee DD1 3BA
Tel: (01382) 434664

Dunfermline
13/15 Maygate
Tel: (01383) 720999

*Edinburgh and Scotland Information Centre
Waverley Market,
3 Princes Street,
Edinburgh EH2 2QP
Tel: (0131) 557 1700

Falkirk
2–4 Glebe Street
Tel: (01324) 620244

Hawick
Drumlanrig's Tower
Tel: (01450) 372547

*Jedburgh
Murray's Green,
Jedburgh TD8 6BE
Tel: (01835) 863435/863688

Kirkcaldy
19 Whytescauseway
Tel: (01592) 267775

*Lanark
Horsemarket,
Ladyacre Road,
Lanark ML11 7LQ
Tel: (01555) 661661

*Linlithgow
Burgh Halls,
The Cross,
Linlithgow EH49 7EJ
Tel: (01506) 844600

Melrose
Abbey House
Tel: (01896) 822555

North Berwick
Quality Street
Tel: (01620) 892197

Peebles
High Street (closed
January–March)
Tel: (01721) 720138

*Perth
45 High Street,
Perth PH1 5TJ
Tel: (01738) 638353

Pitlochry
22 Atholl Road
Tel: (01796) 472215/472751

*St Andrews
70 Market Street,
St Andrews KY16 9NU
Tel: (01334) 472021

*Stirling
Dumbarton Road,
Stirling FK8 2LQ
Tel: (01786) 475019

Other useful Organisations

Forestry Commission
Information Branch
231 Corstorphine Road, Edinburgh
EH12 7AT
Tel: (0131) 334 0303

Historic Scotland
Longmore House,
Salisbury Place,
Edinburgh EH9 1SH
Tel: (0131) 668 8600

National Trust for Scotland
5 Charlotte Square,
Edinburgh EH2 4DU
Tel: (0131) 226 5922

Ordnance Survey
Romsey Road, Maybush,
Southampton SO16 4GU
Tel: 0345 330011 (Lo-call)

For Weather Forecasts

Southwest Scotland
Tel: 0891 232 790

Glasgow and Strathclyde
Tel: 0891 232 791

Edinburgh, South Fife, Lothian and the Borders
Tel: 0891 232 792

East Central Scotland
Tel: 0891 232 793

Grampian and East Highlands
Tel. 0891 232 794

INDEX

Entries in *italic* refer to illustrations.

Abbey St Bathans 44
Abbotsford House 36, *37*
Aberdour 65
Aberfeldy 79
Aberfoyle 71, 73
Aberlady 41
Aberlemno *91*, 92
Abernethy 82
Airth 57
Andrew Carnegie Birthplace
    Museum 62
Anstruther 49
Antonine Wall 8, 58, 60
Arbroath 92
Auchingarrich Wildlife Centre 67,
    68
Auchmithie 90
Auchterarder 76
Avon Aqueduct 18

Balmerino Abbey 83
Balquhidder 68
Bannockburn 59
Barns Ness 45
Barry Mill 90, 92
Bass Rock 40, 41
Ben A'an 70
Ben Lawers 80
Biggar 22, 23
Blackford 55
Blackford Hill 50
Blackness 15
Blackness Castle 16
Blair Drummond Safari Park
    69
Blairgowrie 86
Bo'ness 16
Bo'ness and Kinneil Steam
    Railway 16, *17*
Bonnie Prince Charlie 9, 21, 29,
    56, 75
Borthwick Castle 28
Bowhill House 36
Braco 67
Branklyn Garden 85
Brechin *92*, 93
Bridge of Allan 66
Bridge of Balgie 79
Broughty Castle 90, 92
Bruce, Robert the 8, 25, 34, 59,
    61, 62, 74, 92
Buchanty Spout 75
Burns, Robert 23, 79, 81

Cairnpapple Hill 17
Callander 69, 72
Callendar House 20
Campsie Fells 61
Campsie Glen 60
Carlops 52
Carnegie, Andrew 62
Carnoustie 90
Carnwath 23
Carrington 27, *29*
Carron Valley Reservoir 61
Castle Campbell 56
Castle Menzies 78
Castlelaw Hill Fort 51
Charlestown 20
Chesters, The 41
Clackmannan 56
Clark, Jim 44
Claypotts Castle 93
Cleish Hills 62
Clyde, River 22
Cockleroy 17
Colzium House 60
Comrie 69
Cove Harbour *44*, 45
Craigmillar Castle 27
Craignethan Castle 24
Crail 46, *48*
Crail Museum 47
Cramond Brig 14
Crichton Castle 28, *29*
Crieff 76
Culcreuch Castle 61
Culross 20, *21*
Cupar 49

Dalkeith 26
Dalmeny 14
Dalmeny House 15
Dawyck Botanic Garden 33
Deep Sea World 20
Deil's Cauldron *66*, 67
Dere Street 26, 35
Dirleton Castle *10*, 40
Discovery Point (Dundee) 84, 85
Dollar 56
Dollar Glen 57
Douglas Water 25
Doune 69
Dryburgh Abbey 34
Duddingston 28
Duke's Pass 70
Dunbar *44*, 45

Dunblane 66, 68
Dundee 85, 92
Dunfallandy Stone 88
Dunfermline 62
Dunfermline Abbey 62, *63*
Dunglass Collegiate Church 45
Dunkeld *11*, 89
Dunmore 57
Dunning 77
Duns 44
Dura Den 49

Earn, River 76
East Linton 39
East Neuk of Fife 47
Edin's Hall Broch 42
Edinburgh 6, 12, *13*, 27, 50
Edinburgh Crystal Visitor Centre
    52
Edradour Distillery 88
Elcho Castle 83
Elie *7*, 47
Errol Station Railway Heritage
    Centre 84

Falkirk 20
Falkland *64*, 65
Falls of Acharn 81
Falls of Clyde 24
Falls of Dochart 80
Falls of Leny 69
Fife Ness 47
Fintry 61
Flanders Moss 72
Forfar 92
Forth and Clyde Canal 58, 60
Forth Bridges 21
Fortingall 79, *81*

Garleton Hills 41
Gartmore 72
Garvald 45
Gifford 42, *44*
Gladhouse Reservoir 53
Glamis Castle 93
Glen Devon 55, *56*
Glen Lyon 79
Glen Almond 74
Gleneagles 55
Glenturret Distillery 75, 76
Gullane 41

Haddington 39, *42*, 43
Hailes Castle 38
Harestanes Woodland Visitor
    Centre 35
Hawick 36
Hill of Tarvit 49
Hogg, James 31, 72

Hopetoun House 16
House of Dun 91, 92
House of the Binns 16
Huntingtower Castle *74*, 75

Inchcolm 15, 65
Inchmahome Priory 73
Innerpeffray 76
Inverkeithing 21
Inversnaid 71
Isle of May 49

Jedburgh 36
Jedburgh Castle Jail Museum 37

Kailzie Gardens 30, 32
Keathbank Mill 86, 88
Kenmore 81
Killin 81
Kilsyth 60
Kincardine 57
Kincardine Bridge 19, 57
Kinghorn 64
Kinneil House 16
Kinnoull Hill *84*, 85
Kinross 63
Kirkcaldy 64
Kirkliston 21
Knox, John 43

Lady Victoria Colliery 52
Lake of Menteith 72
Lammermuir Hills 42
Lanark 23
Largo Law 48
Leaderfoot railway viaduct 34
Lennoxlove House 42
Lennoxtown 60
Leslie 64
Lesmahagow 25
Lindores Abbey 83
Linlithgow 17, 19
Loch Achray 70, *71*, *73*
Loch Earn 68
Loch Glow Country Park 62
Loch Katrine 70, *72*, 73
Loch Leven 63
Loch Leven Castle 63, 65
Loch of the Lowes (Borders) 31
Loch of the Lowes (Dunkeld) 88, 89
Loch Tay 80
Lochan na Lairige 80, *81*
Lomond Hills 64
Loup of Fintry 61

Lower Largo 48
Lunan Bay 91
Luncarty 89

MacGregor, Rob Roy 68, 71, 72
Manderston House 44
Mary Queen of Scots 19, 26, 27, 28, 33, 36, 38, 42, 56, 62, 64, 65, 73
Megget Reservoir 31
Megginch Castle Gardens 85
Meikleour 86
Melrose 34
Montrose 91
Muir, John 44
Musselburgh 29
Muthill 77

Neidpath Castle 33
New Lanark 24, *25*
Newtongrange 53
North Berwick 40
North Berwick Law 40
North Queensferry 20

Ochil Hills 55
Ormiston 29

Pease Bay 45
Peebles 32
Penicuik 52
Peniel Heugh 35
Pentland Hills 51, 53
Perth *77*, 85
Phantassie Doocot 39
Picts 8, 82, 88, 92
Pineapple, The Dunmore 57
Pitlochry 89
Pittenweem *10*, 47
Plean Country Park 58
Preston Mill 39
Prestonpans 29

Queensferry Museum 15

Ratho 17
Ravenscraig Castle 64
Reformation, The 8
Restenneth Priory 92
Robinson Crusoe 48
Roslin 27
Rossend Castle 64
Rosslyn Chapel 27, *28*
Rough Castle 59
Royal Observatory, Edinburgh 50

Rullion Green 51

St Andrews 47
St Fillans 68
St Mary's Loch 31
St Monance 47, *49*
Scone Palace 86, 88
Scott, Sir Walter 31, 34, 37, 72
Scott's View 34, *35*
Scottish Fisheries Museum 49
Scottish Mining Museum 28
Selkirk 36
Sheriffmuir 55
Sma' Glen 75, *76*
South Queensferry *14*, 15
Stanley 88
Stevenson, Robert Louis 31, 41, 51, 66
Stirling 8, 56, 59, 68
Stirling Castle 56
Stone of Destiny 8
Strathardle 87, *89*
Stronachlachar 71
Swanston 51

Talla Reservoir 9, *30*, 31
Tantallon Castle 39, *41*
Tay Railway Bridge 83
Tay Road Bridge 84
Taymouth Castle 81
Temple 28, 53
Tinto Hill 25
Torness Nuclear Power Station 44, 45
Torphichen Preceptory 17
Tranent 29
Traquair House 33
Trossachs 70, 72
Tullibardine Chapel 77
Tweed, River 30
Tweedsmuir 31, *33*
Tyninghame 40

Union Canal 19

Vane Farm nature reserve 63

Wade, General George 78
Wade's Bridge, Aberfeldy 78, *80*
Wallace Monument *55*, 56
Wallace's Statue 35
West Linton 52
Whitekirk 40
Wormit 83, *84*

Yetts o' Muckhart 55